GET TO GRIPS WITH

JUDO

GET TO GRIPS WITH

JUDO

Peter Holme

BLANDFORD

First published 1995 by Blandford
A Cassell imprint
Wellington House
125 Strand
London
WC2R 0BB

Distributed in the United States by Sterling
Publishing Co. Inc.
387 Park Avenue South
New York, NY 10016

Distributed in Australia by Capricorn Link
(Australia) Pty Ltd
2/13 Carrington Road, Castle Hill, NSW 2154

**British Library Cataloguing-in-Publication
Data**
A catalogue entry for this title is available from
the British Library

ISBN 0-7137-2516-8
Printed and bound in Great Britain
by the Bath Press, Avon

CONTENTS

Why do I do judo? 'taint no mystery
Need to have a good medical history
My physio told me judo is great
Help them blood cells circulate
Good for the lungs, great for the ticker
There ain't nothin' getcha in better shape quicker
Feels so healthy, feels so sweet
Pulling with my arms, sweeping with my feet
Moulding my muscles, firming my form
Panting like Shire horse sweating up a storm
Keeps me youthful, keeps me loose
Tightens my tummy and shrinks my caboose
Beats being sluggish, beats being lazy
Why do I do judo? maybe I'm crazy!

Anon

ACKNOWLEDGEMENTS

My grateful thanks go to the following people:

Dawn Gunby, who did all the drawings. It is said that 'a picture paints a thousand words'. Dawn has saved me a whole dictionary. It is very difficult to believe she knew nothing of the sport of judo when she took on the job of illustrating my words.

Members of Kendal Judo Club, who patiently posed for the drawings, allowing themselves to be pulled or pushed into the positions I wanted.

Bob Willingham, who spent many hours behind a camera and in the darkroom producing the excellent photographs used in this book.

Tony MacConnell, Dr Ken Kingsbury, Janice Egan, Nicholas Soames and Mick Leigh for their expert opinions and help.

All my many friends and fellow *judoka*, who have added their comments, corrections, amendments, alterations and encouragement to the contents of this book.

Finally, to **Alan Campbell,** my first *sensei* (teacher), who taught me how to play and enjoy the Olympic sport of judo and to whom this book is dedicated.

Domo arigato gozaimasu.

(Note: All references to male players may be taken to include females and vice versa.)

CONVERSION TABLE

1 millimetre (mm)	=	0.03 inch
1 centimetre (cm)	=	0.93 inch
1 metre (m)	=	1.09 yards, 3.28 feet
1 kilometre (m)	=	0.62 mile
1 gram (g)	=	0.03 ounce
1 kilogram (kg)	=	2.20 mile
6.35 kilograms	=	1 stone

Temperature conversion

$$C = (F - 32) \times \frac{5}{9}$$

1 A BRIEF HISTORY OF JUDO

Had an underweight Japanese boy not been bullied at school, the Olympic sport of judo might never have existed. Jigoro Kano was born in the seaside village of Mikage, but his father was promoted to a job in the big city of Tokyo when Jigoro was 11 years old. Undoubtedly the young lad suffered at the hands of the older streetwise kids at his new school.

To overcome this Kano joined two ju-jitsu clubs, one of which specialized in *katame-waza* (grappling techniques) and another which taught only *nage-waza* (throwing techniques). By the time he reached his twenty-first birthday Kano was recognized as a ju-jitsu expert.

Ju-jitsu's popularity rose as a result of the ending of civil war in Japan – the so-called Edo Years. *Samurai* warriors had, for centuries, been well versed in martial arts and were able to use them constantly in war. When peace came, and arms were laid to rest, there was a need to channel this aggressive spirit to something less harmful, especially to the peasants who got in the way of the warriors. Strangely enough, it was a Japanese swordmaster by the name of Ittosai who introduced ju-jitsu as a method of overcoming his opponents without having to draw his sword. However, ju-jitsu was still a rough form of fighting using blows and kicks, and many serious injuries occurred.

Then in 1882 Kano opened his own Kodokan (hall for teaching 'the Way') where he taught his own form of ju-jitsu. He had refined the techniques he had been taught and took out all the blows for safety reasons. He called this refined art judo from the words '*do*' meaning 'the Way' and '*ju*' meaning 'gentle' or 'yielding'. Thus judo or 'the Gentle Way' was introduced to the world. He taught the four objectives of judo, which were 'the study of techniques with which you may kill if you wish to kill, injure if you wish to injure, subdue if you wish to subdue and, when attacked, defend yourself'.

Kano's school or club was successful, beating many of the long-established ju-jitsu schools in competitions. This culminated in a 15-man team of top ju-jitsu fighters challenging Kano's judo pupils. The tournament was refereed by the Chief of Police. The result of 13–0, with two drawn contests, to Kano's Kodokan was so decisive that judo was accepted as part of the Japanese schools' physical education syllabus.

JUDO IN THE UK

Judo was first introduced to the UK as a music-hall act when Yukio Tani arrived at the latter end of 1899 and went on a tour of the music halls, challenging all comers to stay on their feet with him for more than two minutes. There was a handsome reward offered for anyone who could. Tani's skill was obviously great. Despite his height of just 1·57 m, there is no record of him ever being beaten by anyone other than a fellow judo player.

Age and the decline of the music hall made Tani turn to teaching his skills. He joined another Japanese judo expert, Gunji Koizumi, who, on 26 January 1918, opened a club 'for the instruction and practice of Japanese martial arts' in a building near Victoria Station in London. Koizumi called the club the Budokwai (*bu* meaning 'martial'; *do* meaning 'the Way'; *kwai* meaning 'society'). The first members were all Japanese but by March of the same year the first Englishman, O.D. Smith, had enrolled. In April the following year Miss White-Cooper became the first Englishwoman to join.

In a short history such as this it is impossible to mention all the people who contributed to the success of the sport in the UK. However, Gunji Koizumi deserves a special mention (Figure 1 is a contemporary portrait of him when a young man). He is justifiably known as the 'Father of British Judo' and his contribution to the sport cannot be overstated, not just in his teaching of the skill but also in his enthusiasm and boundless energy. He contributed financially too, producing large sums of money to keep the Budokwai and the early British Judo Association (BJA) in funds.

In July 1920, Dr Kano visited the Budokwai and found a flourishing organization teaching not just judo but also kenjutsu (sword fighting), aikijutsu (now known as aikido), ikebana (flower arranging) and chanoyu (tea ceremony). Several important and high-graded judo exponents

FIGURE 1

visited and taught at the *dojo* (literally 'Hall of the Way'). There followed a very close relationship between the Budokwai and the Tokyo Kodokan, which still exists today.

Judogi

The *judogi* or judo clothing was relatively expensive in the early days, with a jacket costing 8s 6d, the tights 2s 6d and the shoes 1s 11d – a total of just under 13s. This was at a time when the average working man's wage was only between £25 and £30 per year.

The first mention of coloured belts to distinguish the pupil from the teacher was in a newspaper article in 1926. According to the writer, the beginner wore a red belt. A sixth Kyu or pupil wore a white belt. A fifth Kyu's colour was yellow, fourth Kyu orange, third Kyu green, second Kyu blue and first Kyu brown. From first Kyu a player went on to become a first Dan – the accepted way of referring to a black belt. In the 1970s this was increased to the current nine Kyu grades, with two grades per colour. Thus a beginner now wears a white belt, ninth Kyu a yellow belt, eighth and seventh orange, sixth and fifth green, fourth and third blue, second and first brown. It is also possible to get a Dan grade in chess or ikebana, or any other Japanese activity.

Judo in the UK expands

By the early 1930s judo clubs were being started in other parts of the UK. These were generally found in towns and cities which had ports. Usually sailors from Japanese ships started them, although members of the Budokwai quite frequently travelled the country encouraging the newly formed societies.

Most of these encouragements were in the form of demonstrations, not just of judo but of other martial arts as well. There had always been such shows of course. The first Budokwai Annual Show took place in 1918. The shows included such wondrous exhibitions as *naginata* (Japanese halberd), *nabebuta* (the use of saucepan lids in self-defence), *kusarigama* (sickle and chain) and *iainojutsu* (the art of sword drawing), as well as judo. These demonstrations continued and increased as the popularity of judo spread. In one year members of the Budokwai undertook nearly 50 such displays, including one at a nudist camp. It was reported that the members returned 'very red-eyed' from the latter.

The clubs so visited were allowed 'to affiliate' to the Budokwai or become associate members. By the late 1930s there were 12 affiliated clubs and a larger number of associates. There were also moves to form a European organization, but these fell through at the start of the Second World War. Indeed the Japanese entry into the conflict almost wiped out the sport completely, although there were small pockets remaining, such as at the RAF station at Blackpool. A member of the British Embassy in Japan, T.P. Leggett, actually practised with his guards during his internment.

Post-war judo

Following the end of the Second World War judo slowly re-emerged as a developing art and by 1948 there were enough clubs to attend a National Judo Conference in London which formed the British Judo Association (BJA). J.G.C. Barnes from the Budokwai was elected as the chairman and G. Hylton-Green from the Imperial College Judo Club became the secretary. Membership was open to all amateur clubs in the UK. The subscription was to be 1s (5p in today's money) per practising member.

A week later a conference of European clubs took place with representatives from Austria, Holland, Italy and France attending. This meeting agreed to form the European Judo Union (EJU), electing Trevor Leggett as its chairman. In terms of progress for international judo it was an amazing fortnight.

The newly formed BJA struggled for several years as many clubs still considered it far more important to be affiliated or associated with the Budokwai. It was not until around 1953/4 that the BJA had more member clubs on its books, at just over 100, than the Budokwai. Nowadays there are close on 1000 member clubs.

The fourth annual EJU conference was

If one picture could sum up the skill, excitement, athleticism and spectacle that is the Olympic sport of judo then this is it. Traineau (France), the under-95-kg world champion, throws Nikas (Greece) in the 1990 European Championships.

held in a Chinese restaurant in Soho, London in 1951. At this meeting, for various political reasons, the EJU was dissolved and the International Judo Federation (IJF) was formed. (The EJU was to be re-formed at an IJF meeting the following year.) The first president was Resei Kano, the adopted son of Jigoro Kano. In 1965 Charles Palmer OBE succeeded Kano and held the office for the next 14 years. It was through his work that judo became a permanent Olympic sport.

THE OLYMPIC SPORT OF JUDO

Men's judo was accepted into the Olympic family in 1964 and, although missing from the 1968 games, it has been a part of the summer games ever since. Women judo players did not join the men until the Barcelona Games in 1992.

Despite never winning a gold medal, when assessed on a ratio of players entered to medals won, judo is Britain's most successful Olympic sport.

In World and European Championships Britons have been reasonably successful, with one men's world champion (Neil Adams in 1981) and several men's winners in the European Championships.

However, British women have had much more success, with a number of world champions. Jane Bridge was the first in the inaugural Women's World Championships held in New York in 1980. Nicola Fairbrother is the current British world number 1, while Karen Briggs from Hull won the World title four times at under 48 kg. Sharon Rendle, also from Humberside, once held the Yorkshire, British, European, Commonwealth and World Championship titles at the same time. She also was a gold medallist at the Seoul Olympics in the same year. However, it was only considered as a 'demonstration sport' in Korea, so she could not, officially, include the Olympic title in that impressive list.

2 PRONUNCIATION AND WRITTEN JAPANESE

DOES THAT SOUND RIGHT TO YOU?

Japanese words are used in judo as an everyday norm. The referee calls instructions during a contest totally in Japanese. It is an easy way of describing a technique, particularly when there is more than one nationality attending your class. I can remember one such group in Corfu where there were eight different countries involved. The instructor was French but the moment he introduced the throw *sode-tsurikomi-goshi,* or sleeve-pulling-hip throw, everyone knew what he meant. He did not have to translate into the other eight languages.

As a referee it doesn't matter that I cannot speak the languages of the competitors. All I need to do is call out in Japanese and they will understand. It matters not if the players come from Russia or Greece, they will all understand me.

As with all representations of another language, especially one which uses a different form of writing, the Japanese words we use in this book are a form of phonetic spelling. In our case the spelling is called *romaji*. Therefore every letter should really be sounded. Different dialects will obviously make the words sound different. The following, therefore, is a general guide to how the Japanese words in this and any other book should be pronounced.

Generally the vowels are short and 'explosive'. 'A' is said as in hat; 'E' as in get; 'I' as in hip; 'O' as in hot; 'U' as in cup. So the throw *seoinage* would be pronounced 'seh-oh-ih-nah-geh'. Occasionally a letter will have a line over the top as in jūdo. This indicates you should lengthen the vowel, thus 'joo-doh'.

There are exceptions. For example the word *osaekomi* should be pronounced 'oh-sah-eh-koh-me'. If said fast the 'AE' is slurred and the word, which is a referee command to start the clock for a hold-down, inevitably sounds like 'oh-sigh-koh-me'. The same sort of blurring takes place with the letters 'S' and 'H', and the following vowel coming together. So Yamashita, the name of the World, Olympic and All-Japan Champion, who never lost a contest in his competitive career, is pronounced 'Yah-mash-ta'.

In Chapter 11 of this book you will find pronunciation hints for all the common words used in judo.

A	I	U	E	O	N
ア	イ	ウ	エ	オ	ン
KA	**KI**	**KU**	**KE**	**KO**	**YA**
カ	キ	ク	ケ	コ	ヤ
SA	**SHI**	**SU**	**SE**	**SO**	**YU**
サ	シ	ス	セ	ソ	ユ
TA	**CHI**	**TSU**	**TE**	**TO**	**YO**
タ	チ	ツ	テ	ト	ヨ
NA	**NI**	**NU**	**NE**	**NO**	**WA**
ナ	ニ	ヌ	ネ	ノ	ワ
HA	**HI**	**FU**	**HE**	**HO**	**WO**
ハ	ヒ	フ	ヘ	ホ	ヲ
MA	**MI**	**MU**	**ME**	**MO**	Lengthens Vowels
マ	ミ	ム	メ	モ	ー
RA	**RI**	**RU**	**RE**	**RO**	Full Stop
ラ	リ	ル	レ	ロ	。

FIGURE 2

KATAKANA

The writing of Japanese is probably different from anything else you will have tried. Before I go into the shapes you can see in Figures 2 to 4, I must first give you a little insight into the history of the Japanese written language.

In the third century the Japanese started using Chinese ideographs, called *kanji*, such as the one to the right, which is the *kanji* for judo. Written properly it has over 20 different brush strokes.

These, as you can see, are very complicated, and represent objects and concepts not sounds. Japanese schoolchildren still have to learn hundreds of these. The advantage is that it is not a spoken language, so people from either end of the Chinese mainland who spoke vastly different dialects, in some cases different languages, could read what was written with equal ease.

At the end of the eighth century, the Japanese began to use a very simple set of ideographs called *kana*. These represented syllabic sounds. That is they are phonetic and represent a consonant plus a vowel. At first this was done mainly for the purpose of writing poetry, particularly by the *samurai* or warrior class. Therefore the sounds of the words were very important.

There are two types of *kana*. *Hiragana* is used mainly for words of Japanese origin and *katakana* for words of foreign extraction. Both have about 80 simple ideographs. Although they are paired with consonants, the five vowels are also given their own character. There is also a separate ideograph for the letter 'N', the only consonant to have this. You will probably be aware that the Japanese language has no letter 'L', so you must substitute the letter 'R' instead.

The Japanese language is one of the most difficult to learn to write. It is a mixture of *kanji* and *kana*. Most ideographs representing objects and concepts such as 'tomorrow', 'judo', 'sugar', etc. are written in *kanji*. However, some, especially foreign words such as 'pen', 'beer' and so on, are written in *kana*. If you think that is difficult – adverbs are in *kana* and adjectives in *kanji* with a *kana* suffix, but sometimes they are all in *kana*. It is the same with verbs.

Personal names are written in *kana*. As yours is a 'foreign' name it will be written in *katakana*. The Japanese use *hiragana* to write their own names.

Are you still with me? Then here is how to write your name in *katakana*. Remember that all the vowels are short. If you want to lengthen the vowel you put a dash '–' immediately after the ideograph. Using the basic 46 *katakana* symbols shown in Figure 2, if you wanted to write 'Susan' it would look like this:

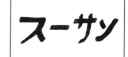

Figure 3 shows some of the basic ideographs which can be changed by the addition of two lines rather like windscreen wipers:

	＼＼

KYA	KYU	KYO	SHA	SHU
キヤ	キユ	キヨ	シヤ	シユ
SHO	**CHA**	**CHU**	**CHO**	**NYA**
シヨ	チヤ	チユ	チヨ	ニヤ
NYU	**NYO**	**HYA**	**HYU**	**HYO**
ニユ	ニヨ	ヒヤ	ヒユ	ヒヨ
MYA	**MYU**	**MYO**	**RYA**	**RYU**
ビヤ	ビユ	ビヨ	リヤ	リユ
RYO	**GYA**	**GYU**	**GYO**	**JA**
リヨ	ギヤ	ギユ	ギヨ	ジヤ
JU	**JO**	**BYA**	**BYU**	**BYO**
ジユ	ジヨ	ビヤ	ビユ	ビヨ
PYA	**PYU**	**PYO**	**WE/YE**	**WI**
ピヤ	ピユ	ピヨ	エ	ヰ

FIGURE 3

The name 'Harry' would look like this:

ハ リ

and 'Barry' would look like this:

バ リ

Figure 4 completes the set of *katakana* symbols, which should give you enough to embroider your name on your

GA	GI	GU	GE	GO
ガ	ギ	グ	ケ	ゴ
ZA	**JI**	**ZU**	**ZE**	**ZO**
ザ	ジ	ズ	ゼ	ゾ
DA	**JI**	**ZU**	**DE**	**DO**
ダ	ヂ	ゾ	デ	ド
BA	**BI**	**BU**	**BE**	**BO**
バ	ビ	ブ	ベ	ボ
PA	**PI**	**PU**	**PE**	**PO**
パ	ピ	プ	ペ	ポ

FIGURE 4

belt. There are only certain parts of the *judogi* which can have embroidery and there is a maximum size as well. The rule says that a *judoka*'s name may be worn on the belt, lower front top of the jacket and upper front top of the trousers, and must be a maximum of 3 x 10 cm.

Your name should really be printed upright, i.e. with the first symbol at the top, like my name printed at the side of this paragraph. However, it is permissible to write it horizontally.

3 BASIC FIRST AID IN THE *DOJO*

INJURIES IN THE *DOJO*

However careful you and the other members of your judo club may be, there will, from time to time, be injuries. Usually these will be of a minor nature, such as the odd sprain, bruise or pulled muscle. However, it is always a good idea for at least one member present at a training session to have some first aid knowledge, including cardio-pulmonary resuscitation. If no one in your club currently has these skills, someone should attend a course.

Contact your local St John Ambulance Brigade, Red Cross Society (or in Scotland the St Andrew's Organization) for details of their courses in the basic procedures for the treatment of injuries. There should also be a good first aid manual in among all those books on judo techniques.

FOOLS RUSH IN

Timing is important in a judo technique. Timing is also important in injury treatment, and usually the quicker the better. However, you should not dive in, grabbing the injured limb, without first talking to the 'patient'. If the player is not in a position to talk (unconscious for example), then the injury is serious and a qualified medical person should be called immediately.

When talking to the injured player ask where it hurts. Can he bend or move the injured limb himself, without any assistance? Does he remember the sequence of events leading up to the injury? Check to see if there is an obvious injury – a dislocation for example. Look at the un-injured limb, and check to see if there are any significant differences between it and the other. Only when you have performed these checks should you start to examine the injury. Look and listen before you touch.

When treating fairly minor injuries think of the mnemonic 'RICE':

R(est) I(ce) C(ompression) E(levation)

Rest

It is important to rest not just the injured part but the whole of the body. This will reduce the pulse rate. The flow of blood to the affected part then decreases, which slows the internal bleeding or bruising, as well as any external bleeding.

Ice

One of the most easily obtainable first aid tools for the immediate treatment of injuries is ice. It is as effective as pain relief sprays and cheaper. It can be kept in a vacuum flask. Some clubs buy out-of-date packs of frozen peas and keep them in an insulated container or fridge. Many clubs are also close to a bar or pub. A friendly word with the landlord will often mean a supply of ice is readily available.

Get the ice working immediately. Don't wait for the bruise to appear. It will be too late by then. Do not apply ice cubes direct to the skin. This will 'burn' it and add to your problems. Wrap them in a wet, thin towel or similar. If no towel is available a plastic bag will do. Leave on the affected part for about 10 minutes until the skin turns bright pink or red. The ice will take away the swelling and reduce the stiffness associated with many limb injuries. If there is still pain reapply the ice after a further 10 minutes, repeating the above instructions. The limb should be raised, if possible, while this treatment progresses.

Ice, when sucked, can also be used for injuries inside the mouth, such as a bitten tongue or cut lip.

Compression

Pressure, correctly applied, can stop the blood flow altogether. However, do not use a tight bandage or tourniquet as this will apply the wrong pressure and may cause further damage. First use hand or finger pressure and then ice.

Elevation

Raising the limb will decrease the blood flow, so preventing bleeding and bruising. However, check for the possibility of broken limbs before you attempt this.

Aspirin is also a good anti-inflammatory treatment. Taken within a couple of hours of the injury it will reduce the pain and inflammation. This in turn helps promote an early recovery of the normal function of the injured part. Check to make sure your 'patient' is not allergic to aspirin, in which case paracetamol is an effective alternative. The use of local anaesthetics (such as a 'PR' Spray') to relieve pain is not recommended.

UNCONSCIOUSNESS

Head injuries are the most common serious judo injury. If a player loses consciousness from a throw, a fall or a blow, proper medical treatment must be obtained immediately. First check very carefully for neck or spine injuries. Only if you are absolutely sure no further damage will occur on moving him, place the injured player in the recovery position (Figure 5). Let him come round on his own. When he recovers consciousness keep him still. Talk to him. Ask him if he can remember what happened, what day it is, where he is. Check his eyes. Are the pupils dilated or of

FIGURE 5

different sizes? These are sure signs of concussion. Is his speech slurred? If in any doubt take him to the local hospital. Whatever the outcome the player should stay off the mat for at least a fortnight. He should also be checked by his doctor before starting training over again.

Unconsciousness from a strangle, contrary to popular belief, is equally serious. Check the player for concussion. Even if there are no obvious signs he should not be allowed to compete or train for at least a fortnight. Juniors should wait longer. Get the player to see a doctor as soon as possible. The player may think it is a waste of time, but it is far better to be safe than sorry.

EXERCISE AFTER AN INJURY

The old adage 'No pain, no gain' is a myth when related to injuries. Pain is your body's warning system. If the pain does not dispel within a couple of minutes then the 'seriousness' of the injury is normally such that a player should rest. Continuing to train or fight is more likely to exacerbate the original problem, which in turn will take longer to heal. It is far better to spend the remainder of the session resting the damaged limb than a month recuperating from an aggravated injury.

During a contest a 'rule of thumb' question would be 'Do you want to continue?' Natural adrenalin will usually make the player say yes. If he says no, the injury is normally one which should cause him to retire or be retired by his coach.

Any injury which has sidelined a player should be rested for at least 72 hours. If there is still severe pain after 24 hours the player should see a doctor. Similarly, if a

complete tear of the ligament, tendon or muscle is suspected, don't wait. See your doctor immediately.

After the three days' rest, movements may be started on the affected part. Keep the movements gentle at first. If the pain starts to become unbearable stop. Wait another 24 hours before trying again. Increase the exercises over the next two weeks. At the end of the fortnight most relatively minor soft tissue injuries will have recovered in a reasonably fit athlete.

PREVENTION IS BETTER THAN CURE

Judo is well down on the list of frequency of sporting injuries. However, it is quite high on lists covering length of recuperation. It is therefore better to prevent them occurring than to go through that long, boring convalescence. Here are some tips to keep you fully active.

1. Always start a training session or competition by 'warming up'. You don't have to do set exercises. Gentle ground-work *randori* for example is just as effective as a routine of press-ups.

2. Having said that, a player should always be looking to extend his range of movement in any part of the body. Exercises such as those described in Chapter 4 should be used for flexibility and increasing mobility.

3. Check the range of movement throughout training. It is better to resolve problems before they start than have to cut back on training because of an injury.

4. Agonists and antagonists (the contractions and counter-contractions of muscle groups) should be well balanced. Both left and right sides should be given equal attention. This means making the flexibility of your naturally weaker side just as important as the normally strong side.

5. Make sure the skill is not too hard for the player. If it is a new technique you are attempting, then the safety angle should be watched closely until the skill has been learned. It is safer if you learn a skill when you are fresh and not at the end of a session when you are tired.

6. Rest should be included in all training programmes. If it is a short training cycle, then one period in five should be a rest. In a long training timetable full-day rests should be included, regularly, in the schedule.

7. Ensure the training conditions are safe. Check equipment (including *judogi*) regularly. Replace anything that is worn or damaged. A large number of injuries are caused through preventable accidents.

STRAPPING UP

Injuries will occur. This is inevitable. However, a long lay-off to repair relatively minor, soft-tissue injuries is inhibiting. Good, well-applied strapping for contests and training sessions will help to ensure that the injury does not get any worse and stays the right side of painful.

Before you get carried away with the strapping read the following. It may save you a lot more aggravation, pain and serious injury.

1. Apply the RICE treatment to any new injury.

2. Have the injury checked by a doctor or properly qualified medical person. There may be a serious underlying injury such as a fracture going unnoticed because of the swelling.

3. Rest the injury for at least a couple of days or longer until the most serious of the swelling goes down.

4. Are you allergic to sticking plaster or similar? If so, put some form of dressing underneath the area you are strapping. This also applies to hairy legs. It gets awfully painful stripping plaster off a forest of hair. An alternative is to shave the legs. Never apply the sticking plaster directly over an open wound. Put some lint on the wound first.

Ankle injury

We'll start with strapping the ankle (Figure 6). The tape used should be about 5 cm wide.

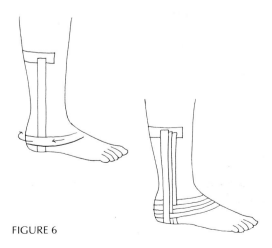

FIGURE 6

23

1. Apply a fixing strip round the lower calf about 10 cm above the ankle.

2. Now place a vertical piece of non-stretch tape, starting from the fixing strap on the inside of the leg, underneath the heel and up the outside to the fixing strap. Meanwhile pull your foot up so the toes are pointing upwards. This will ensure the tape is taut.

3. Still keeping the foot up, place another piece of tape on the outside of the foot just below the ankle. Take it round the back of the heel and bring it round so that it overlaps the first part of the same piece of tape.

4. Repeat 2 and 3 about three or four times, overlapping each piece as you do so. Finally, add another piece of fixing strapping to the finished product to keep it all in place.

5. Do not leave the strapping on when you are off the mat and certainly not overnight. Remember, it is only a training aid. If you leave the strapping on under normal conditions the injury will take longer to heal.

6. Remove the strapping immediately if the pain of the injury increases, the ankle starts swelling again, you get pins and needles in the foot, the joint goes numb, your toes/foot go white or blue, or the leg starts itching under the strapping. All are indications that there is something wrong, so you should stop training immediately and have the leg checked out. It may only be that the strapping is too tight but it is absolutely vital you get someone to have a look at it.

Toes

It is usually the big toe that gets most of the rough treatment. It can get stubbed or caught in the gap between the mats, and however caused it is usually painful. The only way to bring some relief is to use the next toe as a splint. Tape the two together, but remember the warnings I gave in points 5 and 6 above.

Fingers and thumbs

The usual 'minor' injuries to the fingers and thumbs are caused by the opposition pulling his jacket out of your grip. The thumb is particularly prone to dislocation, while fingers usually get muscular injuries.

As with every other injury, get it checked by a suitably qualified medical person. It bears repeating that untreated serious injuries do very rarely mend on their own and those that do always leave that part of the body weak.

Minor finger injuries can be taped in a similar fashion to damaged toes. Using non-stretch adhesive bandage about 2·5 cm wide, tape the injured digit to a sound finger. Do not tape more than two fingers together as this greatly restricts your gripping and doesn't help the injuries anyway.

The thumb is obviously different as you cannot tape that to an uninjured finger. It is also essential for gripping (see Figure 7).

Again use adhesive bandage 2·5 cm wide. Apply two turns round the lower part of the thumb just below the joint. Ideally the turns should go clockwise for the right thumb and counter-clockwise for the left thumb. This makes the second turn come off the thumb and across the palm of your hand. Take it round the back of the hand, round the thumb (from the

FIGURE 7

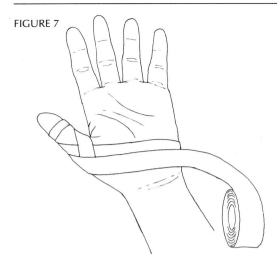

times. You can see this form of strapping in action in the photo on page 56.

Don't forget to remove the tape after the training session/competition is over.

A word of warning about strapping

Go into any judo changing room and you will see players tying themselves together with bandages and sticking plaster. By the looks of some *judoka*, if you untied everything they would disintegrate. All the above strappings I've described are restrictive. They support the injured limb, but by their very nature will not allow full movement. Do not get to rely on such strapping as support, whether mental or physical. Try and use the injured limb/joint normally when not on the mat, and when the damage is healed, throw away the bandages.

bottom of the thumb) and back across the palm. Do this for a couple, maybe three times, then circle the wrist a couple of

4 WARM UP FOR ACTION

Muscles are notoriously lazy. They are quite happy to lie around doing nothing all day if you let them. They are also some of nature's worst whingers. Give them some work to do and they complain. Oh boy, do they complain! Try to make them work without warning and they are likely to go on strike.

This is why, as the boss, if you want to get the most out of your muscles you must gently ease them into work and not crack the whip from the word *hajime*.

It is up to you to decide how you want to warm up. However, you should consider what you are warming up for. Then ensure that those muscles you are going to involve in the exercises are loose and able to go through the range of movements you require. The exercises should cover the full movement range required and then some.

Gentle moving round the judo mat with a partner coming in for throws with little or no opposition is one method. Quiet *ne-waza randori* (ground-work practice), again with a minimum amount of resistance, is another. The *randori* should speed up and get more and more active as the warm-up period progresses.

MOBILIZATION

You need to think about your own requirements when doing a range of exercises. You may have a particular muscle group or joint which requires more persuasion to free itself than others. Your exercises must therefore concentrate on these, perhaps to the exclusion of other parts of you which seem to require no help.

The exercises seen in *dojos* throughout the world are not a haphazard selection of physical tortures concocted by a sadistic *sensei*. They have all been introduced to exercise, strengthen and extend the movements of particular parts of the body most used in judo, and this means all of the body and major muscle groups.

You may or may not want to do the traditional exercises such as cat-dips, leg stretches or sit-ups.

1. Cat-dips (see Figures 8 and 9) make the back supple. From the start position (Figure 8) get your nose to follow the floor until your arms are vertical. Then arch the back. Notice the player is on her toes, which shows that her back is fully extended. This is the whole point of the exercise. Having got to the position shown in Figure 9 the body movement should be reversed rather than just reset to the position in Figure 8.

2. Leg stretches (Figure 10) should start with one player's legs inside the

FIGURE 8

FIGURE 9

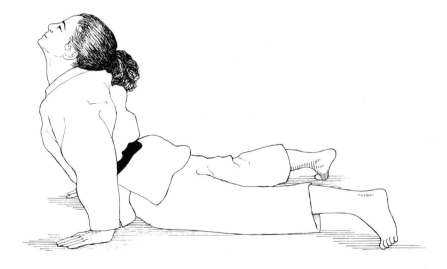

other's. The 'rowing' action should not be a fast action and each player should stretch forwards or backwards as far as is comfortable. Every 20 or so repetitions (or you could use a period of time if there is someone with a stop

FIGURE 10

watch) the position of the legs should be reversed.

3. Sit-ups are a simple exercise. Again they can be done in twos. One player holds the other's ankles. The player doing the sit-ups should have his hands behind his head and, having commenced the exercise, should not allow his shoulders to touch the mat. Having completed the desired number of sit-ups the players swap round.

If your club has gymnasts sharing your premises you could spend an evening watching them practising. You might well discover new ways of extending your range of movements.

There is no doubt that warming-up and mobility exercises can be boring. Why not introduce music into the *dojo* for this? Many traditionalists will not like this suggestion, but music with a strong rhythm is very popular in aerobics and other exercise sessions, and many people find it helps the time pass more quickly. If other members agree to music being played, switch it off immediately the exercising finishes or if other judo activities are going on at the same time. If there are other activities or if other members don't like the idea, you could use a personal stereo.

WHEN TO WARM UP

You should warm up whenever you are about to indulge in a heavy workout. This includes competition as well as training sessions. Training sessions are usually one uninterrupted period. The warm-up will last you through the full period, particularly as you are exercising almost non-stop.

Competitions, however, can have two or three work sessions with long, inactive gaps in between. You should warm up before each round. A great number of pulled muscles occur in the second rounds of tournaments through the player assuming,

28

because he exercised at the start of the day, he had done enough. Sports halls can be cold places and your body cools down very quickly. Find out when you next expect to fight and spend 10 minutes or so before that time going through your loosening-up activities. This also helps concentrate your mind on the contests.

Wear a good, warm tracksuit all the time you are not fighting. A warm body is a relaxed body. Don't forget to wear socks as you lose a lot of heat through your feet and they also go though a great deal of movement when on the mat.

WARM DOWN AS WELL AS UP

Just as important as the warm-up prior to the start of a training session are the warm-down exercises at the end. Fifteen minutes of gentle exercises and joint manipulation at the end of a session will do wonders for your well-being the following day. A warm-down will frequently reduce the aches, pains, stiffness and bruises that often occur, particularly with beginners and lower grades who do not train frequently.

The exercises you do to warm down can be the same as for the warm-ups. Use yoga exercises as well, including short meditation periods. If you are lucky enough to have a practitioner of massage among your members, use him to massage the various muscle groups, particularly the thighs and back.

Remember, 20 minutes spent exercising and warming up could prevent a couple of months off the mat (and possibly off work) with torn ligaments.

5 A NIGHT AT THE *DOJO*

REI (THE BOW)

In fencing each participant salutes the other with his sword; in boxing fighters touch gloves; in wrestling they shake hands; in judo we bow.

There are two forms of bow: the standing bow and the sitting bow (*za-rei*). The first is the one most used and is simply done. Stand with your feet together, hands down by your sides, and incline your body slightly from the waist. It should be pointed out that in Japan the lower you bow the more you are apologizing to the recipient of the bow or acknowledging his

superiority. So in judo just a slight inclination is all that is required.

The sitting bow (Figures 11a and b) is normally used at the start and/or finish of a session when the class thanks the *sensei* or teacher. It is also used during a *kata* performance.

Traditionally there is a correct way to perform this bow. The player lowers himself on to his knees (left knee first), keeping the back upright. He then lowers himself on to his heels, feet together at the back (Figure 11a). Placing his hands, about shoulder-width apart, on the mat in front of his knees, fingers pointing inwards slightly, he brings his head down to just below the

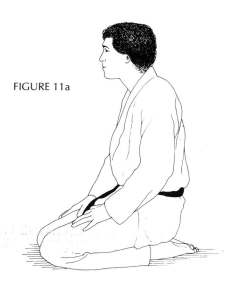

FIGURE 11a

FIGURE 11b

shoulders (Figure 11b). He then comes back to the upright position.

For more on the *rei* in competition, see Chapter 8.

BEHAVIOUR IN A *DOJO*

As you step on to the mat, leaving your slippers by the side, you should make a standing bow. In traditional *dojos* there is always a place for the senior, in rank, members to sit. This place is known as *joseki* and it is these members (whether or not they are present) you are acknowledging. You should always bow to them as you leave the mat as well.

Even in Western eyes it is considered impolite to arrive late for the start of a session. It is inconvenient to all the other *judoka*. Your instructor may be in the middle of teaching a technique and would have to start again if you arrive late.

If you want to leave the mat during a session it is again polite to ask permission from the *sensei* or senior player. You only need to bow to your partner during the *randori* sessions, once at the start of your practice and once at the end. To ask a senior player for a practice, a bow is all that is really required. Under normal circumstances you will not be refused.

At the end of a training session all the pupils should line up along one side of the mat in grade order. The *sensei* kneels opposite. At the command 'Rei' the pupils bow to the teacher and the teacher returns their salutation.

This section may seem old-fashioned to some, but one of the attractions of any of the martial arts is the personal discipline. This is one way the sport of judo keeps the high standards so admired by those in many other sports.

In this part of the book I have assumed that you intend to progress beyond 'recreation judo' and on to the competitive mat.

GENERAL TRAINING PROGRAMME

To get any noticeable effect at all you must train more than once a week. For a club player three times a week should be your target. At least two nights a week should be judo training. Less than this will make little improvement to either your skill or your fitness.

Most leisure centre judo sessions are around two hours long. This can be broken down into several different periods. For the purposes of the timetable below I have assumed that the time allocated for judo is 7.30 p.m. to 9.30 p.m. Of course, if your club is lucky enough to have its own premises this time can be adjusted accordingly.

7.30 p.m. to 7.45 p.m.

Start with warm-up and mobility exercises. Clubs often mistakenly skip this section. This is wrong and is the cause of a number of injuries. I have already discussed mobility exercises and the need for them in Chapter 4. These should be performed, at this level of your judo career, before the start of every session.

7.45 p.m. to 8.15 p.m.

Then go on to the teaching and practice of new skills and techniques. There should be no more than one *tachi-waza* (standing technique) and one *ne-waza* (ground technique) taught. Having been shown the move players should try it out gently. The

31

players do not have to be thrown each time, just lifted off their feet. However, there should always be some completions made in each session. If not you often find novice players get to the point of the throw in a contest then 'lose their way'.

Players should be encouraged, indeed instructed, to try the techniques both left- and right-handed during this period. There is no pressure, as there will be later in the evening, and all competitors should have some 'wrong-sided' techniques in their bag of tricks.

This half an hour can be also used as a gentle warm-up period. It should increase in tempo as the half-hour progresses, with frequent changes of partners.

8.15 p.m. to 8.30 p.m.

In the next 15 minutes move into the more powerful *uchi-komi* (standing practice) with throws included. Again concentrate on the techniques you have been shown that evening. However, as this quarter-hour continues try putting other techniques together with the new throw or ground-work move.

8.30 p.m. to 9.10 p.m.

Next go on to hard *randori* (free-moving practice). This really hinges on numbers and the size of your mat. If you have, say, 20 or 30 players half should be training. Depending on the standard of those on the mat each *randori* period should be two to four minutes long before partners are changed or the second group replace those currently on the mat.

If the mat is big enough all throws should be followed down into *ne-waza*. Those waiting for their turn on the mat should be encouraged to stand guard over those on the ground while they follow up the throw. The players should only be on the ground for 15 to 20 seconds, whether or not they have completed the ground-work move. This ensures a player always has, and uses, a link between *tachi-waza* (standing techniques) and *ne-waza* (ground techniques), and realizes it should be completed quickly.

At least one night a week this *randori* session should be ground work only. It should also be as hard as the standing sessions. More players can practise in these sessions. During the *ne-waza* practices it is important that you aim for a specific objective. Having said that, you should not be so blind as to miss an opportunity to try another type of technique.

In both the standing and ground-work sessions remember it is practice. If the idea does not work out you haven't lost anything. On the other hand, don't give up on an idea if it doesn't work first time – persist.

9.10 p.m. to 9.25 p.m.

The last 15 minutes should be used for a fitness circuit on the mat. See below for ideas on a training circuit for the club player.

9.25 p.m. to 9.30 p.m.

Finally, don't forget warming-down exercises. These are just as important as the warm-up session. Gentle suppling exercises should be used. Many players do not see a need for this last five minutes, but you will find how much less stiff you feel following a heavy session with these few moments of relaxation. A few yoga exercises and moments of silent meditation are not out of place.

TRAINING CIRCUITS

These training circuits are for club-level players. Full-time training sessions are different, and are usually produced on an individual and long-term basis.

Someone should oversee the other club members on each circuit. This means that there is someone to encourage the participants and also to time each period. If the overseer wants to exercise, get another member or spectator to do the timing. The other method is to decide on the number of repetitions of an exercise to be done before a rest.

There are as many different circuits as there are sports clubs but below is a circuit which can be made competitive to improve the performance and there is no need for expensive equipment to perform the exercises.

1. Carry your partner in your arms, like a baby, for 20 seconds up and down the mat. Then your partner carries you while you rest.

2. Carry your partner in a 'fireman's lift'. At the end of each length of mat do a half-squat. Again do this for 20 seconds.

3. Do 'wheelbarrows' with your partner holding your ankles (Figures 12 and 13). Go down one length of the mat

FIGURE 12

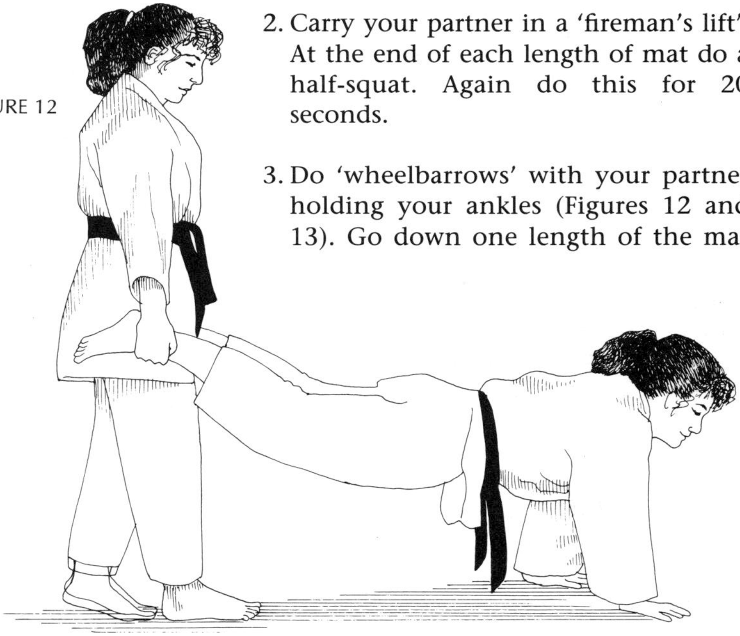

FIGURE 13

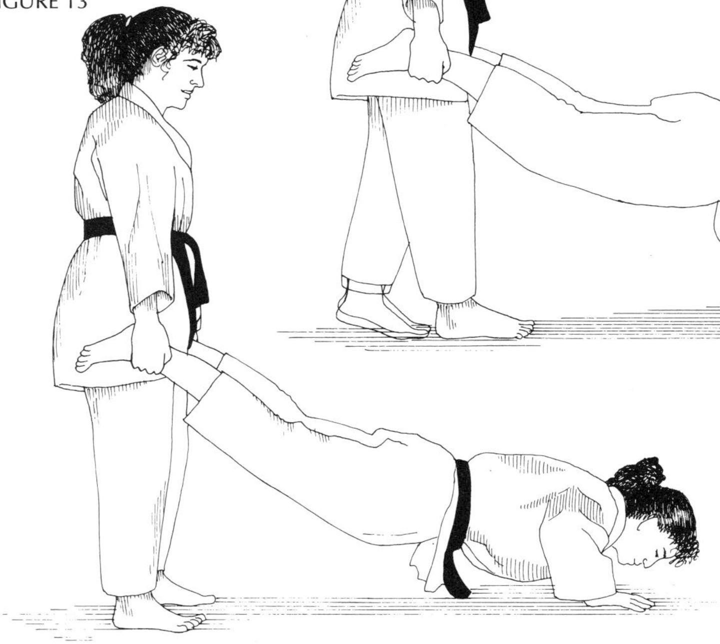

33

non-stop (Figure 12). When you come back, every five steps do five press-ups with your partner still holding your ankles (Figure 13).

4. Perform straight lifts with the elbows (Figure 14). The lifter goes behind the player to be lifted. He is standing with a straight back and feet together. His arms are bent at the elbows, palms up. The elbows are pressed tight in by his side. The lifter, also with a straight back, lifts him off the ground and carries him for 20 seconds.

FIGURE 14

5. Lie on the mat on your stomach. Your partner sits, gently, on the small of your back. You then pull yourself along the ground using your arms only. Beginners or people new to the training should do this exercise without a jockey to start off with

After you have done each activity have a rest while your partner completes the same exercise. Then you move on to the next part of the circuit. Choose your partner carefully for this part of the session, as an over-95-kg player will not make an ideal partner for the under-60-kg player.

When you begin this circuit do it only once for the first two weeks (assuming the three sessions a week). In weeks three and four do the series twice with five minutes' rest in between the two sessions. From week five onwards do three sessions, but increase the distance travelled in the 20 seconds as the weeks progress.

WEIGHT TRAINING

Weight training is for the more advanced player. Again, as with all forms of exercise, you should be supervised. Weights, and their use, are not just a matter of brute strength. Much skill is required to gain the best results from any form of training and none more so than the use of this form of exercise.

Weights should come into your routine when you move up to four and five nights a week training.

PREPARING FOR A COMPETITION

At some stage you will begin to consider entering competitions or gradings. Gradings are a gentle introduction to competitive judo with several advantages for the beginner. First, you will be matched against a player who is around your own skill standard. Secondly, losing a contest will not mean you are automatically out of the event, as can happen in a tournament. You will get at least two fights and quite often more, so if you lose the first contest due to nerves you are still in with a chance of coming away with a prize, i.e. a change of colour for your belt.

No matter what the standard of the event there should be a special build-up for all competitions. Psychologically this gets you prepared mentally as well as physically. The training programme should start about six weeks before the event. Introduce an off-the-mat training programme. For example, before the normal club training those players taking part in a competition should go out on a run. It should be 3 to 5 km long and include some hills as well as flat. Following this run you should start the normal club practice night as I have already described. The run should be timed and students should try to improve their times each night.

The 'competitors' should not rest during the *randori* session. Give them a special coloured belt to wear. All the other club members should then ensure they are not without a partner during that period. This will, along with the run, improve fitness and stamina. The last week of the six-week period they need only do light *randori*.

Introduce 'stress' factors to the *randori*. Try removing your favourite/most successful technique from your repertoire. Try using the skill taught that evening only. When tired you will have to start using skill rather than body weight or strength anyway.

WEIGHT CONTROL

Gradings are not fought in specific weight categories. However, competitions usually are. When you start competing in tournaments, then is the time to become weight conscious. A player should never be more than 2 kg above his fighting weight, once he has started the six weeks' training prior to a competition.

You can reduce weight at the last minute with 'emergency' diets or by sweating it off in a sauna. However, this not only saps the strength you have spent the last few weeks gaining, but you will not know what it feels like to fight at that weight. Fighting at, say, 84 kg is very different from fighting at 77 kg .

This applies especially to juniors. There should be no heavy weight losses permitted with children. The coach should be in control of a child's weight, not the parent. A junior should not have to lose any more than 2 kg at a maximum of 500 g a week. If he cannot do that then he should be moving up a weight in competition. The lower weights in juniors (under 31 kg to under 37 kg) should halve this weight loss and double the length of time it takes.

HYGIENE

Judo is a close-contact sport. It is also a sport requiring a fair degree of exertion which will cause you to sweat. There are therefore several issues which are common sense, but sometimes have still to be said.

When not on the judo mat you should always wear something on your feet, such as a pair of *zori* (slippers), training shoes, or something thicker than socks or bare feet. Similarly, never walk across the *tatami* or judo mat in your outdoor shoes. This is probably considered one of the worst sins in a *dojo*. I can remember a major judo tournament where the guest of honour walked on to the mat to present the medals with his shoes on. Everyone was too polite to say anything, but the intake of breath from the 1000-plus spectators was a more than adequate comment.

Long fingernails can cause some quite serious injuries. Indeed the rule book says both finger and toenails should be cut short. This should apply on the *dojo* mat, as well as in the contest arena.

Make-up, particularly heavy face powder, lipstick and nail varnish, also has no place on a judo mat. Jewellery also should be removed before you step on the mat for safety reasons. I have seen a number of injuries, some very nasty, when earrings or necklaces have been caught as someone is being thrown.

Finally, wash your kit regularly. Too often I have come across *gi* (judo clothing) which could throw me without its partner's help. In *ne-waza* or ground work this is particularly objectionable.

6 IT'S IN THE RULES!

It is the final of the Area Championships. You have worked hard to get there. The referee calls *matte* (wait), as far as you can see, for no apparent reason. Equally amazingly, when you get back to the centre of the mat he gives you a penalty. You are very shocked! You haven't a clue what you have done. Your contest tactics are now much inhibited because you don't want to give any more scores away to your opponent. How you wish you had taken that advertised rules course.

It is not unheard of for a player to blame 'poor and/or biased refereeing', but from 25 years of refereeing experience, I know that most referees would not recognize one player from another, even if they presented their visiting cards at the start of a contest.

So, why must we have rules and referees? Next time you are having a practice at your club get your partner to score each of your attacks/throws and you do the same for him. How many times do you actually agree with each other's calls? You will probably find that it is not very often, hence the need for a referee and rules.

THE RULES AND THEIR HISTORY

1929

Prior to the first international judo contest undertaken by British players in 1929, a list of rules was sent by the Ju-jitsu School of Frankfurt-am-Main in Germany. They included such items as Rule 7 – Every contestant is entitled to the assistance of one second and up to three helpers; Rule 8 – Every contest, if no other arrangements have been made, shall be carried out in three rounds, each lasting three minutes; Rule 13 – The following are allowed: to knock away the hands and feet of the opponent with the flat hand or sole of feet; to bend the fingers or toes in order to loosen the hold.

There was no ban on leglocks or spinelocks, but blows in the tender parts were not allowed.

1951

The Kodokan issued an English translation from the original Japanese rule book in August 1951. There were 36 articles in all. Article 1 stated: 'The Contest Area (*Shiaijo*) shall be a square platform 30 ft in length and width raised 1 ft above the ground.'

Article 10 stated: 'The time limit for the contest shall be from three to 20 minutes. However, the above limit may be extended in special circumstances.' It was not unusual for the referee and judges to declare *hiki-wake* (draw) and give the two contestants extra time to decide the winner. The All-Japan Championship finalists were certainly given 20 minutes, although it was more usual for the major tournament finals to be 10 minutes long.

The number of 'announced' scores had risen to two – *ippon* (one point) and *waza-ari* (near technique). However, there were now another two scores which were not called out. The referee was expected to keep a mental note of them to be included if the scores were equal. They were *waza-ari nichikai waza* and *kinsa*. Having said this, the decision *yusei-gachi* (win by superiority), according to Article 31, '. . . need not necessarily be awarded to a contestant who had been awarded a *waza-ari* if he stalled throughout the match'.

Article 28 listed 21 prohibited acts. Leg and spinelocks had been banned, as had been bending back fingers, but there was no penalty other than *hansoku-make* (loss by violation of the rules).

1972

Just after the Munich Olympics there were major changes in the rules. The powers that be had realized that, to attract sponsors, television viewers had to be appeased. The demarcation line for the edge of the contest area was increased from 7 cm to 1 m. This was accompanied by the re-inforcement of the *keikoku* penalty (equivalent to a *waza-ari* score to your opponent) for going out of the area.

There was also the introduction of two new scores: the *yuko* and *koka*. These were scores that were called and signalled. As a further aid to the competitor, spectator and referee, scoreboards were introduced so that all could see what was going on. There were also lesser penalties of *shido* (guidance) and *chui* (attention) added to the already existing *keikoku* (warning) and *hansoku* (disqualification).

RECENT CHANGES

Changes in judo rules are on-going. They usually happen following the IJF Congress meetings at World or Olympic Championships. Notable among these since 1972 was the introduction of passivity penalties for not attempting anything. In the old days contests could go the full 20 minutes without an attack being attempted. Nowadays inactivity for more than 20 seconds is likely to receive a wind-up, as the passivity penalty is colloquially known.

The head dive, usually from badly executed *uchi-mata* throws (like Figure 15) was, on safety grounds, given a *hansoku* (disqualification) penalty to discourage the technique. Injuries, including paralysis, had been caused throughout the judo world. The idea was successful as the move is rarely seen nowadays, but you will still get disqualified if you try.

Another safety precaution was also introduced. If thrown with a technique like, say, *tomoenage*, it became fashionable to land with head and heels only touching the mat (Figure 16). This was used to try to persuade the referee that, as the player hadn't landed on his back, his opponent could not score. However, this was dangerous as the spine could impact, causing very serious injuries. Referees were instructed to score this as though the player had landed 'normally'. So in our illustration *ippon* would have been called. Had he twisted slightly the referee may have considered a *waza-ari*.

From 1990, five seconds are all a player is allowed in the red 'danger' zone at the edge of the contest area. If he does not attack, or if he does not have to defend from his opponent's efforts, then he will be penalized.

In the early 1990s the IJF have also re-

FIGURE 15

FIGURE 16

The most successful modern-day judo player, indeed some might say the most successful ever – Yasuhiro Yamashita, World, Olympic and All Japan Champion. He has never been defeated in a judo contest. He is seen here attacking with *uchimata* (inner thigh throw) during the 1981 World Championships. (*Colin McIver*)

introduced the non-announced *kinsa* (attack) and allowed *ne-waza* to continue even when more than half a body goes out of the area.

You can see from this chapter that it is worth your while, if you are going to compete on a regular basis, attending referee/rules courses. Next to you the referee is the person most likely to affect your competitive career, so it pays to find out how he will think and react to situations in a judo competition.

JUDO SCORES

Invariably TV commentators, even judo players, describe judo scores in terms of points. For example a *waza-ari* is described as a 7-point score, a *chui* as a 5-point penalty and so on. This causes a great deal of confusion among non-judo spectators. If a *yuko* is worth 5 points, how come two *kokas* (or 3-point scores) do not beat a *yuko*?

The truth is, of course, that only one judo score is worth points: the *ippon* or 1 point. The rest have had these point tags given to them from the system of black belt gradings. In the past points scored in competition were added together and, when a player reached a certain total and took a theory examination, he could change his grade. Players obviously started thinking of every victory in terms of how much closer he was to his black belt. This habit, sadly, has stuck.

For the record no amount of *kokas* equal a *yuko* and any number of *yukos* can be beaten by one *waza-ari*. Two *waza-aris* combine to make one *ippon* (the referee will call '*Waza-ari awasete ippon*', which translates as 'Near techniques joined together make 1 point'). *Ippon*, however it is scored, ends the contest.

Points for wins are considered in two situations: a team competition and when players fight in pools or leagues. Here the end result of a contest is given a points value. Such competitions are first decided by the number of individual wins, no matter how they are scored. If the individual wins are equal between teams or competitors then, and only then, are the points allocated for each type of win added up: 10 points for *ippon*, 7 points for *waza-ari*, 5 points for *yuko*, 3 points for *koka*, 1 point for a win by referee's decision (*hantei*) and no points for a draw/ loss.

The *hantei* point is only valid for an individual competition. In a team event no score or equal scores are given as a draw (*hike-wake*), unless everything else is equal between the two teams. Then the drawn contests are refought and only then is *hantei* given if necessary.

For example, if a player scored a *waza-ari* and his opponent also scored a *waza-ari* this would be a draw or no points. But if one player also scored a *koka* then he

has won by a majority of *kokas*. The win, in a team or pool situation, would be described as a *koka* or 3-point win. Similarly, if a player scored four *yukos* and his opponent a couple of *kokas*, then the player with the *yukos* would be described as winning by *yuko* or a 5-point win, not 4 x 5 = 20 points.

JUDOGI

As I described in Chapter 1, the original *judogi*, consisting of a jacket, belt, a pair of tights and a pair of soft-soled slippers, was comparatively expensive.

Top-of-the-range suits can now cost well over £100, although you may be able to pick up a good suit for £30 or less. This suit, with care and frequent washing, can last you for a long time.

There are strict rules on its size. With the arms stretched out in front of you the end of the sleeve should be less than 5 cm from your wrist joint. Similarly, the bottom of the trousers should be no more than 5 cm from your ankle bone. There must be a space of 10 to 15 cm between the jacket sleeve and your arm, or between the trouser leg and your leg. If you have a bandage or joint support, then that is considered as part of your arm, and the space between jacket or trouser and limb starts from the bandage.

The point where the jacket crosses, *always* left over right (male or female), should have an overlap of at least 20 cm. If yours doesn't, either buy a new jacket or start dieting! The cords which keep your trousers up should tie through the loop at the front. It is amazing the number of people who wear their trousers back to front.

The belt should be long enough to go

twice round the waist, tie in a square knot and leave 20 to 30 cm protruding from each side of the knot. Finally, women competitors should wear a plain, white, short-sleeved T-shirt. Some women may wish to wear leotards but this can produce problems if an injury occurs and the medical person wishes to examine the player. So leotards are prohibited.

'WHAT DID I DO, REF?'

If you intend to compete on a regular basis you should acquire a thorough knowledge of the rules. I cannot emphasize this strongly enough. It is far better to fight 'to the rules' rather than 'within' the regulations. In particular, the section concerned with prohibited acts is a minefield. At the last count there were around 40 individual actions which could be penalized. This includes one which states, 'To take any action which may be against the spirit of judo', thus leaving the book open for the referee to penalize something that does not appear in print. For example, 'Against the spirit of judo' could include running round the mat like a demented footballer who has just won the toss. You should behave with dignity at all times, as this is one of the pluses of judo which should be preserved. A brief description of the prohibited acts is listed below.

Probably the most penalized action, or non-action, is that of passivity. This is followed, particularly in junior judo, with dropping on to your knees. This comes under the heading of 'negative judo'. The referee puts his arms out straight in front and then pulls them down at an angle of about 45 degrees. The actions make it appear as though it is a drag-down he is

penalizing, but it also includes a stiff-armed defence, thus stopping your opponent getting anywhere near you to attempt a technique.

I have seen players lose contests even before they start for the silliest of reasons. The wearing of hard or metallic objects means immediate disqualification. The original rule was introduced to stop players wearing leg braces etc. hidden by their *judogi*. I actually saw an American fighter who had gone on the mat at a British Open Championship wearing such an implement. It was only discovered when she stopped to adjust a bandage. However, this rule also includes gold chains around your neck, rings, earrings, watches, metal staples in hair grips, etc. On another occasion I saw a top French player lose her place in the Olympics because she forgot she was wearing a chain around her neck when she went on for a contest and was disqualified. It is always best to divest yourself of any jewellery for the day just in case.

A brief guide to the rules

The current rules cover something like 56 pages. This is too much to be included in this book but a copy can be obtained from British Judo Association Head Office, 7a Rutland Street, Leicester LE1 1RB.

There are nearly 40 things you're not allowed to do on a judo mat during a contest.

Like the official rule book, I've grouped them together under the penalties they are most likely to receive for the first offence in a contest. However, it is possible that the referee could give a harsher punishment if it was thought that you deserved it.

If a player is given a *shido* penalty,

which gives his opponent an automatic *koka*, and then does something that would normally be given a *shido*, the referee has to hand out a *chui*, the next penalty up. The *koka* is removed from the scoreboard and is replaced by a *yuko*.

If you've got a *shido* and you do something to be penalized with a *chui* then it's a *chui* you get. A *shido* plus a *chui* does not make a *keikoku*. However, a *chui* followed by a *shido* does make a *keikoku* and a *waza-ari* score to the other player.

Shido

So, what do you have to do to get a *shido*?

1. Deliberately avoid taking hold of your opponent.

2. In *tachi-waza* (standing techniques), hold the belt or the bottom of the jacket without attacking. Similarly, hold the same side of the jacket or one sleeve with both hands. Be caught holding your opponent's sleeve ends or screwing them up as a defence. In all of these the referee will consider a penalty after five seconds.

3. Interlock fingers (yours and your opponent's). This will attract attention after five seconds as well. Nor can you put your fingers up the inside of your opponent's sleeve or trouser leg. However, you can put them up your own sleeves or trouser legs.

4. Not make a positive attacking move for 20 to 30 seconds. This is likely to be the shorter time earlier in the day as referees tend to be a little more sympathetic the further the competition progresses. This is known as passivity and the referee

indicates this by rotating his hands round each other.

5. To be excessively defensive in a standing position. It is known as *jigotai*. There is a five-second time limit on this, after which expect a penalty. A typical example would be stiff, straight arms, or bent double or almost double and thereby not allowing your opponent an opportunity to attack.

6. Try to fool the referee into thinking you are attacking, but have no intention of actually attempting a throw. This is known as a false attack.

7. Stray, with both feet, into the red 'danger' area and then fail to attack the other player or defend against your opponent's attack for five seconds. The referee will hold one hand up, fingers spread apart as he points at you, and say the dreaded word *shido*.

8. Using your *judogi* in various ways is also frowned upon. For example, deliberately and obviously disarranging your *gi* and tying or untying your belt, without first getting the referee's permission, is worth a *shido,* so is totally encircling any part of your opponent with your, or his, belt or jacket. Only half circling round will bring no response.

9. You are not allowed to put your opponent's or your own *judogi* in your mouth. Nor may you put your foot in your opponent's belt, collar lapel or face. Actually putting anything across the other player's face (the normal hairline, down to the chin and from ear to ear across) will be penalized.

10. If you take a hold of a leg then you must be attempting a throw. If not it's a *koka* to your opponent and a *shido* to you.

11. Finally, if you are holding round the neck or shoulders of your opponent with your legs and he gets to his feet you must let go. Otherwise you know what will happen, or should do by now!

Chui

Next come the *chui* penalties. There aren't as many of these, but don't forget that 2 x *shido* = 1 *chui*.

1. We'll start this section with a relatively new addition to the rules. You cannot apply a *shime-waza* (strangle technique) using a belt or bottom of the jacket.

2. If your opponent has got you in a strong grip then you can't bend back his fingers, or kick his hand or arm with your knee or foot in order to make him let go. Although it is not actually written down, hitting him with your hand is not allowed either.

3. Another dangerous action is to apply leg scissors to either the trunk or the neck. This is a misunderstood rule. The wording actually says, 'to apply the action of *dojime*', which means crossing your feet while stretching out the legs and thereby applying considerable pressure. There is nothing to stop a player from crossing his legs as long as no pressure is applied.

4. If you want to take your opponent

into *ne-waza*, because you have invented this devastating hold-down, then you must use judo. To drag him down with little or no finesse will just get a *matte* call and a penalty. This applies even if your opponent takes advantage and turns you into a hold, except that the referee won't call *matte*.

5. Finally, for *chui*'s sake stay inside the contest area. If you go outside the fighting area when attempting an attack you run a great risk of a penalty. If the referee believed it was a deliberate exit then the penalty could be higher than the *chui*.

Keikoku

This brings us to the serious stuff. A *keikoku* is the equivalent to a *waza-ari* to your opponent, which is not a position you really want to be in.

Most of these penalties are for actions which could seriously injure a player and the high penalty is to discourage the actions that might cause such an incident.

As hinted in the last paragraph of the previous section, if the referee believes you deliberately went outside the contest area or forced your opponent to go outside the area (without actually attempting a judo technique) you will be given a *keikoku*. Similarly, having gone outside the area, for whatever reason, applying any technique will incur the official's wrath.

1. You may not apply *kawazu-gake*, which, simply described, means entangling your leg round your opponent's then falling backwards on him. Also applying *kansetsu-waza* (jointlocks) to any

part other than the elbow is a 'no no'. Neck or spinelocks, or anything else which could injure those parts of the body, are specially checked.

2. You are in a semi-standing position and your opponent underneath is applying a *shimewaza*. If you can get to your feet and lift your opponent off the ground, the referee will call *matte*. Put him back down gently. Slamming him back into the mat will get you a *keikoku*.

3. Applying an armlock, particularly a standing version of *waki-gatame*, while you are, at the same time, attempting to throw your adversary gains you a penalty and your opponent a *waza-ari*.

4. A move which is not seen often, although it is usually the lower grades who 'accidentally' try it, is sweeping away, from the inside, the supporting leg of a player who is attempting a 'one-legged' throw such as *harai-goshi* or *uchi-mata*.

5. Ignoring the referee and any of his instructions, and mouthing off at your opponent, will be bound to get you a penalty.

6. There is one other *keikoku* penalty which covers a multitude of sins. I quote it in full: 'To make any action which may injure or endanger the opponent, or may be against the spirit of judo.'

Hansoku

Finally we come to the instant disqualification.

1. To dive head first on to the mat while attempting such throws as *uchi-mata* etc. (as in Figure 15).

2. To deliberately fall backwards while your opponent is clinging on to your back.

3. Last, but by no means least, is to wear hard or metallic objects. As I have said, this rule was introduced to stop people wearing such things as leg braces, but even the smallest staple in a hair grip can be, and has been, interpreted as metallic.

7 JUDO TECHNIQUES FOR WINNERS

Before I start describing the judo techniques in this chapter there are a couple of points I would like to make.

First, the aim of a book like this is to show you the basics – your ABC. Then, metaphorically, with a good coach you will be able to sit down in front of a word processor and use that alphabetical knowledge to write a book. A good judo coach will be able to turn a well-executed basic technique into something which is unique to you alone.

Secondly, except for identical twins, no two judo players are alike. Even including the twins no two competitors ever throw, hold, strangle or armlock the same. A 1·8 m, 95 kg male competitor will attempt *seoinage* (shoulder throw) in an entirely different manner to a 1·5 m , 47 kg woman.

Despite the differences, there is a right and a wrong way to perform a technique. The basic points have to be there for it to succeed. The adaptations made because of weight, height, age, experience, etc. will help you, the individual. This is the work of a coach.

I am right-handed, but in most cases my descriptions can be simply reversed for the left-handed player. Where this is impracticable I will describe the left-handed movements as well. Incidentally, it is not against the rules for a left-handed player to attack right-handed or vice versa.

Indeed, it is good practice to be able to perform both left- and right-handed versions of any technique.

O-SOTO-GARI – MAJOR OUTER REAPING

This is a technique that is attempted frequently by the lower grades. Almost as often it does not succeed. The beginner decides it is too difficult and drops one of the most spectacular throws in the book from his very small portfolio. By so doing he usually loses 50 per cent of his rearward throws. Women attempt *o-soto-gari* even less, usually because it looks like a 'brute strength and ignorance' technique. How looks deceive!

There are five main stages in most techniques. In this throw they are as follows:

1. **Balance of your opponent** To attack a leg that is 'loose' (i.e. no weight on it) is a complete waste of time. It is simplicity itself for your opponent to step off the throw and turn your attacking motion into impetus for his counter-technique.

   Pull your opponent strongly round to your right. In most cases he will resist. Use that resistance by pulling sharply sidewards and slightly down-

FIGURE 17

wards with your left hand (Figure 17). At the same time your right hand should lift slightly with the forearm pushing hard into the chest. (Look also at the photo on page 48.)

2. **Use your movement to keep him off balance** While all this is going on, your left foot should step forward strongly just outside and slightly behind the plane of your opponent's right leg. At the same time your right leg should drive across and down the back of your opponent's right thigh, as high up, to start with, as possible.

3. **Drive off the left foot** Your head should be over the driving left leg. You should be pushing hard with the left foot (Figure 18). It sometimes helps to hop forward on this foot.

FIGURE 18

Onda (Scotland) attacking Price (Wales) during the under-71-kg category of the 1992 Scottish Open.

4. **Don't stop the right leg's movement** Having started the driving action downwards with the right leg, now change the movement to an upwards sweep. As much as possible keep your opponent's and your thighs in contact (Figure 18). That right leg should be travelling upwards for as long as it takes to put your partner on his back.

5. **Upper body contact** Keep your upper body in full contact with your opponent's at all times. This will prevent him from twisting out of the throw. Your grip of his jacket must be strong. The pull with the left hand and the pushing of the right must be constant throughout the throw.

Why does this technique fail so often?

1. **Opponent's weight not on the leg being**

attacked This is usually caused by a weak pull with the left hand or because you haven't manoeuvred your opponent into the 'right' position. A good entry into this throw can come from a strongly defended *harai-goshi* (sweeping hip) attack (see photo on page 48). Your right leg is usually in the right place for the attack. The defence from your opponent, provided you are attacking hard enough, means he will shift his weight backwards off your hips trying to twist out of the throw. This puts him in the position described in point 1 above.

2. **Left foot and head not far enough forward** You usually discover this error as your opponent counters your attempt with an *o-soto-gari* of his own. If you haven't got that left leg behind your opponent and your head at least in a perpendicular line with your foot, you are leaning backwards. This is what you have been trying to do to him. Is it any wonder he takes advantage of this and throws you?

3. **The right leg is not high enough up your opponent's leg** This is particularly important if your opponent has longer legs than you. If you only catch the calf with your leg and continue to sweep, an agile opponent can swing his leg off yours and turn into something like *harai-goshi*.

4. **The right leg stops moving** This is often as a result of point 3, usually because it comes in contact with the mat. Having stopped, your opponent's left leg can step back. He can regain his balance and come in with his counter-attack.

5. **Drive from left foot fails** Point 2 is usually the cause of this, although it is sometimes because you are flat-footed. The only way to get committed drive is to come up on to the ball of your foot. If you are flat-footed or, even worse, if your weight is on your heel, you are likely to be leaning backwards.

Practice always makes perfect. However, you do not have to throw your partner every time. Practise everything as hard as possible, but instead of catching your opponent's thigh with your right leg just sweep up alongside. Miss him by the thickness of his *gi* only.

Try also using moving *uchi-komi*. Get your partner to walk slowly towards you. As you progress down the mat first just practise stopping his movement and getting his weight on to the correct leg. Then add your own attacking movement with your left leg. Follow this with the full technique again using the 'airsweep' until the last attempt as you arrive at the end of the mat. Then you throw him.

SOTO-MAKIKOMI – OUTER WINDING THROW

The photo on page 50 shows a classic version of this technique. Instead of attacking with the standard two-handed grip *uke*'s (the player who is being thrown) right arm has been pulled across *tori*'s (the player executing the technique) body.

Having trapped this arm, a very strong rotation by *tori* pins *uke* on to the foot which is about to be swept away as in the normal *o-soto-gari*. You can also see in the photo the point I made earlier about the attacking foot/leg continuing its upwards movement as long as the opponent is still

Van de Cavaye (Belgium), the 1993 World Champion at under-61-kg, throwing Arak (Poland) with *soto-makikomi* (outer winding throw) during the 1994 European Championships.

Van der Lee (Netherlands) holds Cicot (France) with *ushiro-kesa-gatame* (reverse scarf hold) to win the 1994 European Championships.

upright. If she is lucky the player in the white suit will get away with *waza-ari*. Even if I were a betting man I wouldn't put much more than 10p on that. My 50p would be on an *ippon* score being given by the referee.

USHIRO-KESA-GATAME – REAR SCARF HOLD

This is another 'classic' technique that appears in the Kodokan *gokyo* (the traditional 'Five Courses of Instruction').

Having been out of favour for some time it is now back winning contests. See the photo above, which shows Monique van der Lee winning the 1994 European Championships with this technique.

Like most *ne-waza* there are numerous ways of getting your opponent into the hold. Here is the traditional beginner's method. From there on in you should practise as many different ways as possible. The important point of this entry is that it gives you an indication of just how important the holding of the left arm is.

Entry

This is a good practice entry. A similar opportunity could well occur in low-grade contests, but the higher the grade the less likely it is you will be given such an easy opening.

1. *Tori* is on all fours in a defensive position (Figure 19). *Uke* attacks, attempting to pull him over or get a hold of the collar for a strangle.

FIGURE 19

2. *Tori* grabs the arm or wrist and rolls over to his left. As he traps that left arm by his side *tori* should reach over and hold on to *uke*'s belt with his right hand (Figure 20).

3. As he does this *tori* pushes his elbow up into *uke*'s armpit.

4. A tight grip on his own collar by *tori* will make it very difficult for *uke* to pull that hand out. However, the main reason for the success of this hold is the pressure applied to the ribcage. This makes it very difficult for *uke* to breathe.

5. To increase the pressure *tori* should turn his body to the right (towards *uke*'s head). There is nothing so de-

FIGURE 20

moralizing as someone turning to smile at you as you are fighting for just a couple of millilitres of oxygen.

Escape

Uke usually spends the first few seconds trying to ease this pressure. If he turns in towards *tori* the pressure increases. Turning away from his opponent is difficult unless he can leave his arm behind. Applied properly the only chance to escape is to get that left arm free. It is not a totally impossible feat but there are only 30 seconds to succeed.

The first cause for *uke* escaping usually happens almost before the hold is thought of.

1. As *tori* rolls, *uke* pushes his right arm under *tori*'s right armpit. The roll, which tori probably cannot stop, now turns him on to his back and into an equally rib-crushing hold. To avoid this *tori* should pull his right arm tight into his side or even underneath his chest.

2. Having turned his opponent into the hold *tori* shuffles around to get into a more comfortable position for him. This shuffling will ease the pressure.

If it is uncomfortable for you it certainly isn't a bed of roses for your opponent. It's only 30 seconds and you're on top.

3. *Tori*'s legs should be at a fairly safe distance from *uke*'s, or at least he should be aware of the potential life-giving escape he will get, should *uke* manage to trap *tori*'s legs in his. The referee must call *toketa* (hold broken).

4. A slack hold on the left arm will allow your opponent to break free. Once that happens the hold is no more. Do not panic! You can still keep the *osaekomi* (holding) going by changing to a new hold.

Just before I go on to the next hold, the entry described above is not cast in stone. In your next *ne-waza randori* session you should be able to find other, perhaps easier ways of getting into what is a very strong hold.

MUNE-GATAME – CHEST HOLD

As you can see from. Figure 21 there is a fairly simple transition from *kuzure-kesa-*

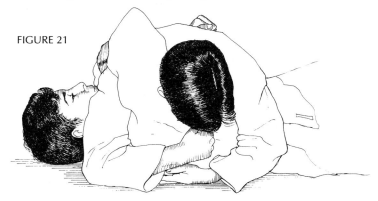

FIGURE 21

gatame into *mune-gatame*. Just roll over and trap your opponent's right arm. However, you've got to be quick.

1. Like most hold-down techniques you must trap at least one arm and prevent it from having free movement. It will, in most cases, have some activity, but as long as it just flaps around where you want it to it doesn't matter.

2. The important point about this, one of the simplest holds in the book, is the lifting of *uke*'s shoulder blade off the mat surface. It is now difficult for him to roll because he has nothing to push against.

3. Let your opponent roll in towards you. As he does so, wrap your arms underneath the point of his collarbone, the further under the better.

4. Now push your legs as far back as they will go and try to push the front of your hips through the mat. Ideally, the pressure should be put on the lower half of the ribcage which will apply more pressure to the diaphragm.

5. Finally keep your head down. Bear in mind the minus points.

   (a) Not putting enough pressure on the chest by relaxing the hips or not pushing the legs far enough back. I have often seen players attempting this technique on their knees. You are giving your opponent too much room to twist and turn.

   (b) Lifting your head to look at someone at the mat side could allow that right arm to come round your neck. Your opponent will then have a lever

in order to attempt a strangle.

(c) Not keeping your body at right angles to your opponent. This could give him an opportunity to trap your legs in his as in the first hold-down.

(d) Allowing the shoulder to get to the mat surface. Now your opponent has a lever from which he can twist, turn and generally make your life, or at least the next few seconds, very difficult.

UDE-GARAMI – ENTANGLED ARM

This *kansetsu-waza* (locking technique) is more commonly known as the 'figure-four lock'. (A look at Figure 22 will make its name clear.) This technique is not at the height of its popularity, although it has had its moments. It is not an easy armlock to apply as there is a great deal of suppleness, particularly in women, in the arm and elbow joint. However, given a sharp, accurate action it can still be a match winner.

Version 1

1. As you can see from Figure 22 *ude-garami* can easily be applied from a failed attempt at *mune-gatame*. The accuracy needed for this armlock is in applying the pressure to the elbow joint, not the upper or lower part of the arm. Smack in the middle is where the pressure is required.

2. *Tori*'s right forearm, the bony side uppermost preferably, should go directly under *uke*'s elbow. To either side will require a great deal of pressure to make the technique succeed.

FIGURE 22

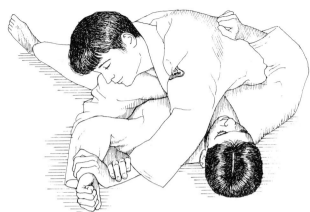

3. The attacker's left arm should grasp the wrist of his opponent. If he can flatten the back of the wrist on to the mat surface so much the better.

4. With his right hand grasping his left wrist *tori* now raises his right forearm sharply, keeping *uke*'s wrist on the mat. At the same time he should try and keep pressure on *uke*'s chest because one way of relieving the pressure is to bridge and twist the body towards the arm being attacked.

5. If the initial attack does not work then *tori* should pull the arms, still keeping his under *uke*'s elbow, towards *uke*'s side and apply the upwards pressure again. This frequently brings an instant submission.

But it can all go wrong. You can get an opponent who has 'rubber' arms. This particularly applies to women, who seem less susceptible to armlocks than men. If it is not working quickly check the following.

1. Is your arm under your opponent's elbow? If it is under the upper arm you might, in the opinion of the referee, be applying a shoulderlock, a possible *keikoku* penalty.

2. Is the back of the wrist flat on the mat? Often when applying the lift *tori* relaxes and allows the wrist to come up. This negates the whole armlock.

3. Can you pull the whole entanglement closer into *uke*'s side? Try and keep the figure-four shape as you do this and lift your right arm sharply.

4. Collapse the bridge as soon as *uke* attempts it. Move the lower part of your body a bit closer to his head, making more weight for his neck to support.

5. Be prepared to change back into *mune-gatame* if your opponent's arm is bending too much.

Version 2

This comes from a failed *kesa-gatame* (scarf hold).

55

Del Columbo (France) holding Selin (Finland) with *kesa-gatame* (scarf hold) during the 1989 World Championships.

1. First of all, why has the hold failed? If you look at Figure 23 you will see that *tori* is holding *uke* in *kesa-gatame*, but his head is too far back. It should be down close to his opponent's head and over the shoulder/arm he has trapped.

2. If you can, try and get your right knee underneath *uke*'s shoulder blade (see photo above). This gives him less of a lever to twist out of the hold.

3. Your left arm should be trapping *uke*'s upper right arm. *Uke*'s elbow should be behind your arm. When *uke* starts to try and pull his arm out he has got to

FIGURE 23

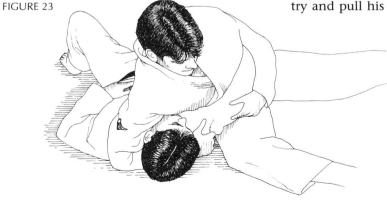

make space for the bulge of the elbow to come out easily. A tight grip makes this difficult. In Figure 23 the player underneath has almost got his arm free, just like the photo on page 56.

4. Keep your trunk across *uke*'s chest diagonally (hence *kesa* – see Chapter 11) and be prepared to move your right hand to prevent your opponent twisting to his left.

Several things have gone wrong in Figure 24 and a good *uke* will use this weakness to get that right arm free. If he does, it can

give you an opening for a second version of *ude-garami*.

1. Instead of trying to fight the arm back into the *kesa-gatame* position grasp the wrist. Push the arm straight down (Figure 24) with the upper part of the leg underneath the elbow. You might just get an *ippon* submission there and then if you push it down sharply enough.

2. *Uke*'s arm is fairly strong and he will obviously be trying to relieve the pressure by bending the arm the natural way. Quickly release the downward force and, as the arm comes up,

FIGURE 24

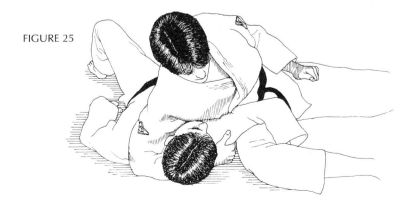

FIGURE 25

put *uke*'s hand/wrist under the calf of that right leg (Figure 25).

3. You now have a form of *ude-garami*. To apply more pressure try pushing your right hip forward.

4. If that doesn't succeed, put that head down and hang on with *kesa-gatame*. *Uke* now has another problem to worry him as he tries to get out of the original *osaekomi*.

5. As with all armlocks it should be applied quickly and sharply. Many players can stand a great deal of discomfort if an armlock is put on slowly and gently. However, do be a little more careful when you are practising these during a training session. Remember it is his turn next to try!

   Still not working?

   (a) Move the right leg so that the thigh comes under the elbow.

   (b) Push the right hip forward a bit more and lift the thigh a little.

   (c) Move the lower part of the leg or bend it a bit more.

   (d) Lower the head and left shoulder. It doesn't seem to be much but it certainly helps.

Version 3

This last version is not to get a score but will give you a chance of getting out of a tricky situation.

In this instance *tori* is on his back with *uke* on top. *Uke* reaches forward, perhaps with the intention of attempting a strangle. *Tori* grabs *uke*'s wrist from the underside with his left hand. The right arm goes quickly under *uke*'s elbow, grasps his own wrist on the top and pushes sharply away from him.

This is unlikely to get a submission, but it doesn't half give *uke* a shock! While he is recovering *tori* has a few more seconds to think of a way out.

SODE-JIME – SLEEVE STRANGLE

There is a *shime-waza* (strangle technique) known as *hadaka-jime* which uses bare arms. Its English translation is 'naked neck lock'. However, to use it properly you need to attack your opponent from behind. This opportunity rarely comes in judo contests. Most other strangles in judo use the jacket and require a player to be either on top or underneath. There is little room for manoeuvre. This strangle is one which keeps on surfacing on the contest mat and can be attempted from just about any angle and any position. This includes standing as well as ground work.

I've given it the title of *sode-jime* (sleeve strangle), but it might even be called *sode-guruma-jime*, for you wheel (which is what *guruma* means) an arm around the neck. However, there is already another strangle with that name, so *sode-jime* will do.

My illustrations have *tori* underneath but he could just as easily be on top or even standing. Whatever the position the application is the same.

Tori takes an arm (right or left) round the back of *uke*'s neck. He should make sure the jacket sleeve goes as well (Figure 26a). His other hand takes hold of the sleeve. It doesn't matter if it is inside the sleeve because it's his own sleeve and you are only penalized when you hold the inside of your opponent's sleeve. Keeping

FIGURE 26a   FIGURE 26b

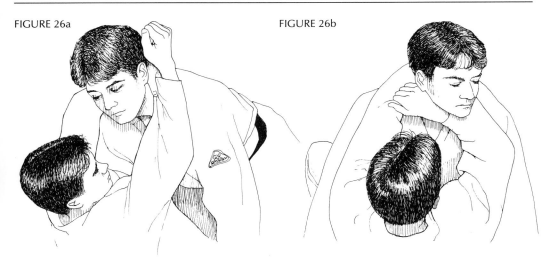

a strong hold of the end of the sleeve, bring the arm which is inside the sleeve back round, under the chin and grasp the outside of the other sleeve (Figure 26b). Now just pull on one or other of the sleeves. This is a very strong strangle from which it is difficult to escape.

1. This has to be applied quickly. Any hesitation and your opponent will slip your arms over his head and the opportunity is lost.

2. The hand which grasps the sleeve end must have a strong grip for there is a great deal of pressure applied when this strangle goes on. An inside sleeve grip is usually the strongest.

3. Again, the reason for speed is apparent when the next part of the move is made. A quick *uke* will sink his chin into his chest. Now you have a problem. If you have read the 'Prohibited Acts' part of your Rule Book you will know that it is an offence to put an arm, or leg, across

your opponent's face. It matters not that he put his chin there.

4. All is not lost, however. If you follow the line of the collarbone round with your thumb you will find a soft piece of flesh which will allow that hand to get under that defensive chin.

5. The bony part of the wrist should be pressed into the side of the neck. The carotid artery comes down either side of the neck just about where your wrist will be. Having got to this position pull with the other hand, thus applying pressure with the edge of the sleeve on the other side of the neck as well.

6. If you cannot get the hand underneath the chin, be very careful where you put your hand. The referee will always be looking for that hand across the face. The moment he spots that it will be *matte* and a penalty for you.

Having got the basics correct for all these

techniques now try your adaptations. Pick a taller/smaller/lighter/heavier partner and see how you have to adjust. Practise moving your opponent from all angles so he is in the 'right' place for your attack. Try the attack from different positions. See which attacks work and which don't. Don't be afraid to experiment but make sure you have the proper framework to start with.

8 COMPETITIONS

PREPARING FOR A COMPETITION

In order to compete at an event you must first of all enter, preferably in plenty of time. That may seem like an obvious statement to make. However, I wish I had £1 for every phone caller I've listened to at midnight (and later) asking if it is too late to enter a competition starting at 9 o'clock the following morning.

Secondly, read the entry form. Make sure you are entering the correct category and you know what time weighing in and booking in are. If you are delayed, for whatever reason, it is always worth stopping for two minutes to make a phone call to the venue. It might save you a long journey for nothing if they cannot hold things up for you. Most organizers will try and help, provided they know about it. Turning up two hours after booking in has closed and expecting to fight is not the best way to endear yourself to a competition controller.

Your weight

Do you know what weight you are? No, don't go digging out the bathroom scales from under that sweaty *judogi*. If you are starting to get serious about competitions you should keep a close check on your weight. See Chapter 5 on training for more on this.

It's funny how the scales used at competitions are always inaccurate. It is also most peculiar how they never register your weight as being lighter than it should be. You are always heavier. Isn't that strange? It couldn't be your scales that are wrong, could it?

Go on, humour me! Check how accurate your bathroom scales are. Go along to Boots or a chemist with a public weighing machine. They are obliged to check its accuracy regularly. Weigh yourself, then go straight back home and check what your own scales say. Adjust them or take into account the difference. Do this on a regular basis.

AT THE START OF A COMPETITION

Listen for your category being called. If there is a timetable check the time you are expected to start fighting. Always anticipate beginning at least half an hour earlier. I can remember a player missing out on a European Championship place because he thought that the previous group would overrun. They sometimes do, but don't count on it.

When called, ensure the official in charge of the mat knows you are there. If you must go to the lavatory ensure the same official knows about it and knows when you are back.

These are simple things, but many players have lost the chance of a medal because of such mistakes. Remember, if you fail to turn up for a contest, any contest, you will be eliminated from the competition. There is no appeal.

Starting a contest

Tradition and respect for your opponent have a great deal to do with how to start a contest. This applies to any contest, be it a grading or the World Championships.

Come on to the contest area from the side. Bow as you step on to the contest area. Walk to the mark on the mat (red or white depending which colour belt you are wearing). Bow again and take one step forwards. Your opponent will have done the same. When the referee says 'Hajime' (begin) you start to fight.

The procedure is exactly reversed at the end of the contest. You stand one pace inside the mark. As the referee indicates the winner (you, I hope!), you take one step back and bow. You then walk to the edge of the contest area and bow towards the centre of the mat as you leave it. Wait for your name to be called out again.

This is a simple process, but one which seems to give a large number of players, not just beginners, a great deal of trouble.

The bow (rei) used in all contests is the standing bow (Figure 27): feet together, hands by your sides. Incline the upper half of your body slightly, then straighten up. Simple? Don't go overboard. In Japan the larger the inclination of the body the greater the apology you are making for your existence.

FIGURE 27

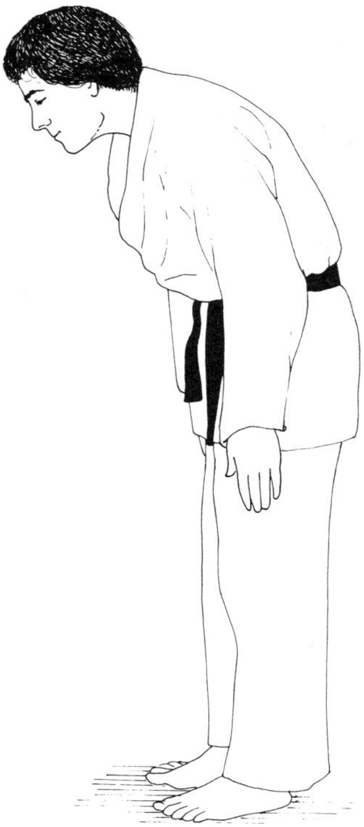

TYPES OF COMPETITION

There are five main types of individual competition in judo.

The knockout

Competitors are paired off. The winner of each pairing goes forward to meet another winner from a similar couple. This proceeds until there is just one player left who has not lost a contest. He is the winner. Usually the pairings are written out right from the start. You can follow who will fight whom right the way through to the final.

The repêchage

The knockout is run as above. Then all those beaten by the two finalists have another knockout competition to find who wins the bronze medals. The first-round loser fights the second loser. The winner of that contest then fights the third loser and so on. The repêchage is fought for both sides of the knockout, thus producing two bronze medallists.

Pools throughout

This is not a common form of competition. The competitors are arranged into groups or pools with three or four players in each. There can, in some circumstances, be five. Each player fights all the others in his pool. The winner is the player with the biggest number of contest wins. If those are equal then the points are counted up: 10 points for an *ippon*, 7 for *waza-ari*, 5 for *yuko*, 3 for *koka* and 1 point for a *yusei-gachi* (win by decision). The player with the highest number of points is declared the winner. If two are equal then the result of the contest between those two drawn players is used to decide who has won.

Normally the top two players from each pool go through to the next round when the procedure is repeated. However, if two players who have already fought each other meet up again in a later round, the result of the original contest is carried forward and they do not fight again.

Pools to knockout and repêchage

This is a combination of the first three types, with the pools used as a first-round elimination. This is the usual method used in club and area competitions. This time, if two players meet a second time – this will only be in the final – they fight again. The result of the first round is not carried forward.

Knockout and compound repêchage

This is similar to the normal repêchage, except all players, once defeated, come back into the repêchage at the point where they are defeated. Again, if two players meet for a second time they fight again. This should only be in a fight for a bronze medal.

9 KATA –
PREARRANGED JUDO

Kata, which translates properly as 'forms', is probably the most neglected side of judo in the modern practice of the sport. The common translation of *kata* as 'a formal demonstration' probably gives an instant, though incorrect, mental picture and may well also give a reason for its lack of popularity. Practised and performed correctly, however, *kata* can be an entertaining and instructive training aid.

The original object of a *kata* is to provide *tori* (the thrower) with a predetermined set of movements by his partner, *uke* (the receiver), so that he, *tori*, can practise the relevant skill without having to concern himself with the position of his opponent as in *randori*. *Tori* can therefore concentrate on the technique exclusively and thereby improve his technical ability.

In theory a *kata* demonstration can comprise any number of techniques of any description, provided you can prove a link between the techniques in your *kata*. However, in practice there are 10 recognized *kata* in judo. These were formalized at a meeting in the Kodokan, Tokyo, Japan in 1960 and are:

1.	*Nage-no-kata*	'Forms of throwing'
2.	*Katame-no-kata*	'Forms of grappling or holding'
3.	*Go-no-sen-no-kata*	'Forms of counters'
4.	*Kime-no-kata*	'Forms of self-defence'
5.	*Goshin-jitsu-no-kata*	'Forms of modern self-defence'
6.	*Ju-no-kata*	'Forms of gentleness'
7.	*Itsutsu-no-kata*	'Forms of fives'
8.	*Koshiki-no-kata*	'Forms antique or ancient forms'
9.	*Joshogoshinho-no-kata*	'Forms of self–defence for women'
10.	*Seiryokuzenyo-kokumin-taiiku-no-kata*	'Forms of physical education based on the principles of maximum efficiency'

The last five of these, the most esoteric, are now rarely performed. However, the first five *kata* still have a useful role to play in modern judo, as well as a link with the more traditional sport envisaged by Jigoro Kano.

Kata in other oriental martial arts is usually the basis of all training from the beginner upwards. In judo this form of training is usually not introduced into the player's knowledge until he is attempting promotion to black belt (first Dan). This is a pity, for *kata* is another opening to players who are not keen on, or who have no inclination for, contest judo. There are *kata* competitions which are marked on the correctness of the presentation. The performance has to be very stylized, with little room for improvisation, but nevertheless requires a great deal of skill to perform.

Provided a good instructor is found and it is introduced to a *judoka's* training programme early in his career, *kata* can still be used as an important training aid.

THE *KATAS*

Of the five *katas* still in regular use the first two are performed frequently, particularly as they are required knowledge for promotion to and within the Dan grades.

All should be performed correctly. The performance starts from the moment the players approach the mat. It includes bowing to *joseki*, as well as each other in *za-rei*.

Nage-no-kata

This is split into five groups of three throws. Each group comprises a specific type of throw.

Group 1. *Te-waza* (hand techniques):

uki-otoshi (floating drop);
seoi-nage (shoulder throw);
kata-guruma (shoulder wheel) (Figures 28a to d).

Group 2. *Koshi-waza* (hip or loin techniques):

uki-goshi (floating hip);
harai-goshi (sweeping hip);
tsurikomi-goshi (lifting pulling hip).

Group 3. *Ashi-waza* (leg and ankle techniques):

okuri-ashi-harai (sliding sweeping ankle);
sasae-tsurikomi-ashi (propping drawing ankle);
uchi-mata (inner thigh).

Group 4. *Masutemiwaza* (rear sacrifice throws):

tomoe-nage (high circle throw, better known as stomach throw);
ura-nage (rear throw);
sumi-gaeshi (corner throw).

Group 5. *Yokosutemiwaza* (side sacrifice throws):

yoko-gake (side dash);
yoko-guruma (side wheel);
uki-waza (floating technique).

All except one of these techniques are performed on the right, followed immediately by the same throw shown on *tori's* left side. The odd one out is *uki-goshi*, where the left-hand version is performed first. In general the lead-up to each technique is done in a stylized way. For example, eight of the throws use a form of foot movement known as *tsugiashi*. One foot is used as the leading foot, while the trailing foot is brought up to within centimetres of the leading foot before it

FIGURE 28a

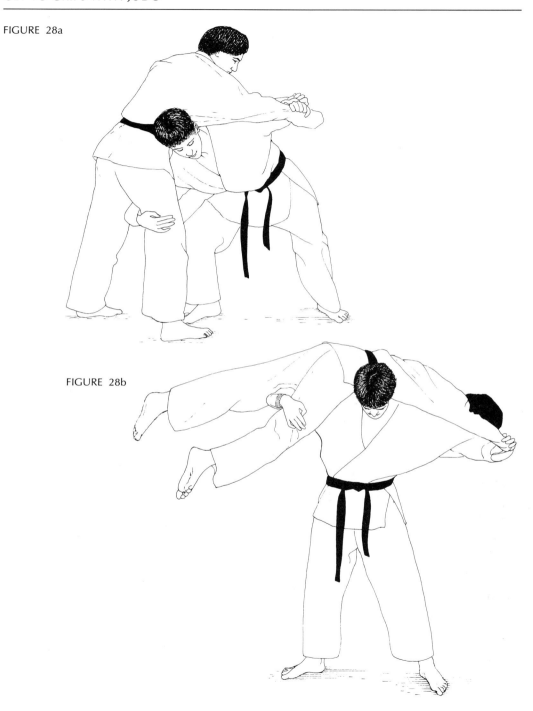

FIGURE 28b

FIGURE 28c

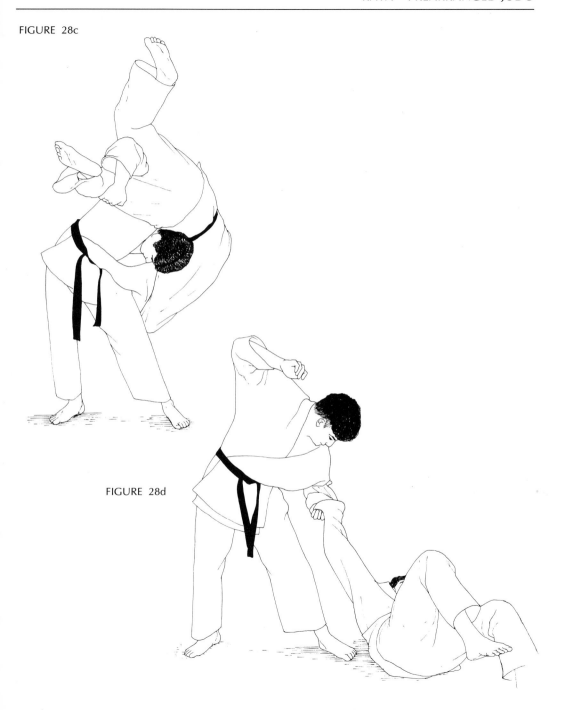

FIGURE 28d

makes the next step. The feet do not cross at any time as in normal walking.

Katame-no-kata

This is split into three groups of five techniques. As in *nage-no-kata*, each group is of a specific type of technique.

Group 1. *Osae-waza* (holding or pinning techniques):

kuzure-kesa-gatame (broken or variation of scarf hold);
kata-gatame (shoulder hold);
kami-shiho-gatame (upper four quarter hold);
yoko-shiho-gatame (side four quarter hold);
kuzure-kami-shiho-gatame (broken or variation of upper four quarters).

Group 2. *Shime-waza* (strangle techniques):
kata-juji-jime (half cross strangle);
hadaka-jime (naked neck strangle);
okuri-eri-jime (sliding collar strangle);
kata-ha-jime (single wing or shoulder strangle);
gyaku-juji-jime (reverse cross strangle).

Group 3. *Kansetsu-waza* (armlock techniques):

ude-garami (entangled or figure-four armlock);

juji-gatame (cross armlock);
ude-gatame (forearm armlock or arm crush);
hiza-gatame (armlock using knee);
ashi-garami (entangled armlock using leg).

Go-no-sen-no-kata

In this *kata uke* attacks *tori*, who uses the attack as part of his counter-attack eventually to throw *uke*. The *kata* contains 12 attacks and their respective counters.

Kime-no-kata

This is a self-defence *kata*. The techniques are split into two groups. The first *idori* (kneeling techniques) has eight different exercises. The second *tachiai* (standing techniques) has 12 exercises.

Goshin-jitsu-no-kata

This is another self-defence *kata* which, when it was originated in 1958, was considered suitable for men only. There are 21 routines in all: seven grappling or wrestling techniques; five when the two performers are apart; three when *tori* is 'attacked' by someone holding a dagger; three when *uke* has a stick; and three when *uke* is holding a pistol.

A full study of the *katas* is a specialized subject, requiring a book of its own.

10 DRUGS IN SPORT

THE BASICS

The many questions asked by sports people, coaches and parents regarding drug abuse show a need for simple information on drugs testing in sport, banned drugs and alternative medication for minor complaints.

Definition

Doping is defined as the taking or use of substances or participation in doping methods prohibited by the International Olympic Committee (IOC) and by international sports federations. In addition, assisting or inviting others to contravene doping regulations is also an offence.

Say 'no' to drugs

Drug abuse must never become the norm in sport. It harms health and deforms the values which participation in sport can give. Sports people can take drugs simply to cheat or be persuaded into taking drugs by others. They may also take banned drugs by mistake. We should all welcome the rules and testing that can deter cheats, protect people from undue pressures and educate against mistakes.

BANNED DRUGS AND HARMFUL EFFECTS

Banned substances are grouped into various types, as follows:

1. anabolic agents and testosterone;
2. growth and peptide hormones;
3. beta blockers;
4. diuretics;
5. narcotic analgesics;
6. stimulants;
7. blood doping;
8. pharmacological and chemical manipulation of blood.

Types 1 and 2 are used medically to recover strength and growth in genuine medical conditions. They are not used medically by healthy sports people. They cannot be obtained over the counter by mistake or without a prescription. A very serious view is taken if these are found in a player's sample.

Anabolic agents include androgenic anabolic steroids, which are the drugs most people refer to as 'steroids' when talking of doping in sport. However, there are other agents such as Clenbutarol which are also banned.

Among the harmful effects of anabolic

steroids and testosterone are stunted growth, a damaged liver and masculinisation in women.

Growth and peptide hormones can cause allergic reactions and acromegaly (enlargement of the bones, particularly in the hands, feet and face), and should never be used without a medical reason.

Beta blockers are used to control the heart rate in cases of heart disease. They modify the heart rate and are dangerous in such a highly active sport as judo.

Diuretics are used, medically, to increase the excretion of urine. Like types 1 and 2 these cannot be obtained from a chemist without a prescription. There is no medical need for their use in healthy men, but some women retain fluid before menstruation which can cause general discomfort. If diuretics are prescribed for women in such cases, great care must be taken in their consumption before competitions.

Using diuretics, like other attempts at dehydration (fluid restriction, excessive saunas, etc.), can be dangerous. If wrongly used they can lead to weakness, nausea, kidney damage and heatstroke.

Narcotic analgesics are strong painkillers, and include morphine and like substances.

Strong painkillers are dangerous when competing or training. They can mask damage and lead to more, serious injury. Dependency on this type of drug often leads to inadequate or improper treatment of injury. It can also mean a player becoming addicted to the substance in more serious cases.

Stimulants include amphetamine, ephedrine, pseudoephedrine and caffeine. Some are used medically to relieve bronchial problems and as a nasal decongestant for colds.

Stimulants, in general, accelerate the heart and constrict blood vessels. They also increase hostility and competitiveness. This reaction can, and quite often does, lead to loss of judgement. This, in turn, can lead to accidents. Amphetamines and similar compounds have caused death in high-activity sports. There is no reason for their use in any sport.

Narcotic analgesics and stimulants need care. They often require a prescription. However, they can also be found in ordinary cures for coughs, colds, hay fever, asthma and upset stomachs, to name but a few. These can be bought over the counter. The most common banned substances are ephedrine, pseudoephedrine and phenylpropanolamine. You should take great care when buying any form of over-the-counter 'cure'. If in doubt check with your doctor, chemist, the governing body of judo or the Sports Council.

It is well known that caffeine is present in coffee, tea and some soft drinks such as Coca-Cola. The permitted level in the urine will not be exceeded by normal drinking on competition or pre-competition days. However, it is better to quench your thirst with water or fruit juice, or one of the sports drinks.

Blood doping is the artificial increase of blood oxygen levels in an athlete by transfusion. Again, as in most forms of this type of cheating, there is no medical reason for this in a fit person, male or female.

The obvious dangers of doping include acute anaemia, kidney damage, jaundice, hepatitis and even Aids.

Ignorance is no defence

Because a drug or a form of illegal doping is not mentioned in this chapter it does not mean you can try it out. There is a whole industry producing new substances every week to help cheats find their way to the winner's rostrum. The Medical Commission of the IOC regularly update the list of prohibited substances. The current list can be obtained at any time from the Sports Council Doping Control Unit, Walkden House, 3–10 Melton Street, London NW1 2EB.

Not knowing you are taking an illegal substance is not a defence for a positive test either. The only way of being certain is not to take anything unless you know it is legal. If a stranger should offer you a tablet, pill or injection, simply say no!

ALTERNATIVE REMEDIES

If medication is needed while training or competing there are alternatives to banned drugs. Some of the many examples are as follows.

1. Colds: aspirin, paracetamol, menthol inhalant, Karvol.

2. Coughs: menthol inhalant, Benylin Chesty Cough, Copholco.

3. Headaches and other pain: aspirin, paracetamol.

4. Sore throat: soluble aspirin, paracetamol gargle, TCP.

5. Dyspepsia/nausea: anti-acids, Maxolon, Stemetil.

6. Diarrhoea: fluid replacement, Kaopectate, Lomotil.

7. Asthma: Intal, Ventolin, Pulmadil, Becotide inhalers.

8. Hay fever: antihistamines, Rynacrom, Beconase, Otrivine.

9. Allergies/insect bites: antihistamines.

10. Travel sickness: Sturgeon, antihistamines, Sea-legs.

Antibiotics and oral contraceptives are also allowed. Anti-inflammatory agents such as Nurofen, Brufen and Froben are permitted at present. In general it is better not to use medication at all unless it is genuinely needed.

DISCIPLINARY ACTION

The disciplinary action taken when a positive test is found depends, among other things, on the substance taken. However, the British Olympic Association (BOA) has a rule regarding positive tests. Put simply it says that anyone found guilty of a drug-abuse offence in any sport will not be allowed to compete in any Olympic Games.

DON'T EVEN THINK ABOUT TRYING DRUGS. THE CONSEQUENCES CAN SERIOUSLY DAMAGE YOUR SPORT-ING CAREER AS WELL AS YOUR HEALTH.

11 JUDO TERMS
THEIR PRONUNCIATION AND TRANSLATION

I will begin with a reminder of the pronunciation. Generally, vowels are short and explosive sounds. The letter 'A' is pronounced as in hat (except at the start of a word, when it changes to something like the 'U' in hut); the 'E' as in get; the 'I' as in hip; the 'O' as in hot; and the 'U' as in cup (except where I have put a macron above the letter thus – Ū. It is then pronounced like the double 'O' in boot).

Japanese word	Pronunciation	Translation
arigato	ari-ga-toh	thank you
ashi	ash-ee	leg or foot
ate	ah-teh	hit or strike
atemiwaza	ah-teh-me-wa-za	punching technique
awasete	ah-wah-seh-teh	joined together
būshido	boo-she-doh	way of the warrior
chūi	chew-i	(lit. attention) a penalty equivalent to a yuko score to a player's opponent
Dan	dan	(lit. step) a black belt judo grade. Black belts go from first Dan to, theoretically, twelfth Dan; tenth Dan is the highest ever awarded
de	day	advance or advancing
do	doh	'the Way', as in judo – the Gentle Way
do	doh	the trunk of the body
dojo	doh-joh	(lit. the Hall of the Way) a place where judo and other martial arts are practised
domo arigato	doh-moh-ari-gah-toh	thank you very much
eri	eh-ri	neckband or collar of the jacket
fūsen gachi	foo-zen-ga-chi	win by non-appearance of a player's opponent
gaeshi	ga-eh-shi	to counter; sometimes spelt kaeshi
gake	ga-kay	hook or block
garami	ga-rah-mi	entangle or wrap
gatame	ga-tah-may	(lit. to harden) to hold
go	goh	five, fifth

Japanese word	Pronunciation	Translation
go	goh	an ancient Japanese territorial board game
go-no-sen-no-kata	goh-noh-sen-noh-ka-ta	forms of counter-techniques (see Chapter 9)
goshi	goh-shi	hip; also spelt koshi
goshin jitsū	goh-shin-jit-soo	self-defence
gurūma	guh-roo-mah	wheel; also spelt kuruma
gyaku	gee-ya-kuh	reverse
hachi	ha-chi	eight, eighth
hadaka	ha-da-ka	bare or naked
hajime	ha-ji-may	begin
hajimemashite	ha-ji-may-mash-teh	good morning. Greeting used up to around 10 a.m. See also kombanwa and konnichiwa
hane	ha-neh	spring or jump
hansoku	han-soh-kuh	disqualification. A penalty equivalent to giving a player's opponent an ippon win
hantei	han-teh-i	judgement or decision asked for by the referee when the scores are equal at the end of a contest. The judges raise a red or white flag according to whom they consider has won
hara	ha-ra	abdomen or belly
harai	ha-ra-i	sweep; sometimes spelt barai
hidari	hi-da-ri	left as opposed to right
hiki	hi-ki	pull; sometimes spelt hikki
hiza	hi-za	knee
hon	hon	basic
ichi	i-chi	one, first
ippon	i-pon	one point. The ultimate score in judo
itsūtsū-no-kata	it-soot-soo-noh-ka-ta	forms of five. A series of techniques demonstrated together in a very formalized manner (see Chapter 9)
jigotai	jih-goh-tah-i	defensive attitude/posture
joseki	joh-seh-ki	place of honour in the dojo where guests or the most senior players sit during a training session. A player should always bow to joseki when stepping on to a mat as a mark of respect. If there is no physical joseki it is usually accepted as being directly opposite players as they step on the mat
jū	joo	ten, tenth
jū	joo	gentle, as in judo 'the Gentle Way'. Gentle in this instance means giving as a willow tree gives and bends to the force of a strong wind
jū	joo	gun
jūdo	joo-doh	the Way of Gentleness (see above)

Japanese word	Pronunciation	Translation
jūdogi	joo-doh-gi	clothing worn to practise judo. Comprises a jacket, trousers and a belt. Sometimes abbreviated to gi
jūdoka	joo-doh-ka	someone who practises judo
jūjitsū	joo-jit-soo	Japanese self-defence art, the forerunner of judo. It is an art which is still practised
jūno kata	joo-noh-ka-ta	forms of gentleness. A demonstration of techniques which highlight 'giving way' (see Chapter 9)
kaeshiwaza	ka-eh-shi-wa-za	counter-techniques. See also gaeshi
kai or kwai	k-eye	society or club
kake	ka-keh	the point where a throw takes effect
kami	ka-mi	hair
kami	ka-mi	paper
kami	ka-mi	upper
kansetsūwaza	kan-set-soo-wa-za	locking techniques. Applies to all joints but only those against the elbow joint are allowed in judo
kao	ka-oh	face
kata	ka-ta	form. A very formalized demonstration of a set of judo techniques (see Chapter 9)
kata	ka-ta	shoulder
katsū	kat-soo	resuscitation. Usually used to bring round players unconscious from a strangle. Uses points on the body, rather like acupuncture but without the needles
keiko	keh-i-koh	training, practice
keikoku	keh-i-koh-koo	warning. A penalty which gives opponent a waza-ari score in a judo contest
kesa	keh-sah	a monk's sash which is worn diagonally across his chest
kiai	ki-ah-i	a shout used to help exert maximum effort
kikengachi	ki-ken-gah-chi	win due to opponent withdrawing during contest because of injury
kime-no-kata	ki-meh-noh-ka-ta	forms of decision or actual fighting (see Chapter 9)
ko	koh	ancient
ko	koh	arc
ko	koh	minor
Kodokan	koh-doh-kan	the spiritual home of judo. The headquarters of judo in Tokyo, Japan
koka	koh-ka	(lit. effect) the lowest score which appears on a scoreboard. Usually described as 'almost yuko'

Japanese word	Pronunciation	Translation
kombanwa	kom-ban-wah	good evening. Greeting used after dusk. See also *hajimemashite, konnichiwa*
konnichiwa	koh-ni-chi-wah	hello. Used after 10 a.m. until dusk. See also *hajimemashite, kombanwa*
koshiki-no-kata	koh-shi-ki-noh-ka-ta	forms ancient (see Chapter 9)
koshiwaza	koh-shi-wah-zah	hip techniques
kūbi	koo-bi	neck
kumikata	kuh-mi-ka-ta	gripping, taking hold
kuzure	kuh-zuh-reh	to break or broken
kuzushi	kuh-zuh-shi	to disturb the balance of a player
kyū	ki-yoo	nine, ninth
kyū	ki-yoo	pupil grade in judo. The *judoka* who wear coloured belts
ma	mah	exactly
makikomi	mah-ki-koh-mi	(*lit.* to wrap up) commonly known as 'winding throw' (see photo on page 50)
masūtemiwaza	mah-soo-teh-miwa-za	rear sacrifice technique
mata	mah-tah	upper/inner thigh
matte	mat-teh	wait. Referee's instruction. Temporarily halts the contest and brings both players back to the centre of the contest area
migi	mi-gi	right as opposed to left
mon	mon	(*lit.* gate) in British judo it is applied to junior *judoka* grades. The belt colours are the same as the senior Kyu grades but there are three grades per colour. These are indicated by red stripes at the end of the belt
morote	moh-roh-teh	two hands
mune	muh-neh	chest
nage	nah-geh	throw
nage-no-kata	nah-geh-noh-ka-ta	form of throws (see Chapter 9)
nami	nah-mi	normal
nami	nah-mi	in line
nana	nah-nah	seven, seventh; sometimes the word *shichi* is used
newaza	neh-wa-za	(*lit.* lying-down techniques) ground techniques
ni	nee	two, second
o	oh	major
obi	oh-bi	belt or sash
okūri	oh-koo-ri	sliding
osaekomiwaza	oh-sah-eh-koh-mi-wa-za	holding technique. The referee calls '*Osaekomi*' to indicate to the timekeeper that the hold is on

Japanese word	Pronunciation	Translation
otoshi	oh-tosh-i	drop
randori	ran-doh-ri	free-moving practice
rei	reh-i	bow
renrakuwaza	ren-rah-kuh-wa-za	combination technique
renshū	ren-shoo	practice
renzokūwaza	ren-zoh-koo-wa-za	linking or linked technique
roku	roh-kuh	six, sixth
ryū	ree-oo	school
ryū	ree-oo	dragon
samurai	sah-muh-rye	ancient Japanese warrior
san	san	three, third
sasai	sah-sigh	propping
sayonara	sah-yoh-na-ra	goodbye. Used informally among friends
sensei	sen-seh-i	teacher
seoi	seh-oh-i	carry on the back
seoinage	seh-oh-i-nah-geh	normally translated as shoulder throw, but this is not quite correct
seppūkū	sep-poo-koo	the proper word for ritual suicide usually, wrongly, referred to as 'harakiri'
shi	she	four, fourth; sometimes the word *yon* is used
shiai	shi-aye	contest
shiaijo	shi-aye-joh	contest area
shichi	shi-chi	seven, seventh; sometimes the word *nana* is used
shido	shi-doh	(*lit.* guidance) penalty equivalent to a *koka* score for a player's opponent
shihan	shi-han	founder
shiho	shi-hoh	four quarters
shime	shi-meh	tighten
shime	shi-meh	strangle
shita	sh-ta	underneath
shizentai	shi-zen-tie	natural standing posture
sode	soh-day	sleeve
sogogachi	soh-goh-gah-chi	a win in a contest where one player is penalized by *keikoku* and his opponent then scores a *waza-ari*. Equivalent to *waza-ari-awasete-ippon*
sonomama	soh-noh-mah-mah	(*lit.* as it is) referee's word to freeze the actions of the players during a contest
soremade	soh-reh-mah-deh	(*lit.* that is all) referee's word to end a contest
soto	soh-toh	outer or outside
sūkūi	soo-koo-i	scooping

Japanese word	Pronunciation	Translation
sumi	soo-mi	corner or angle
sutemiwaza	soo-teh-mi-wa-za	(*lit.* throwaway technique) normally translated as sacrifice technique. A player sacrifices his standing position (i.e. throws himself to the ground) in order to throw his opponent
tachiwaza	ta-chi-wa-za	standing techniques
tai	tah-i or *tie*	body
tani	ta-ni	valley
taniotoshi	ta-ni-o-tosh-i	valley drop (a sacrifice throw)
tatami	ta-tam-i	straw mats used as floor covering in Japanese houses. Also used as mats in *dojos*. Although the originals were made from rice straw the word *tatami* now generally refers to any type of judo mat
tate	ta-teh	length
te	teh	hand
tewaza	teh-wa-za	hand technique
tekubi	teh-koo-bi	wrist
toketa	toh-keh-ta	referee's call to indicate that a player has escaped from a hold-down (*osaekomi*)
tokuiwaza	toh-koo-i-wa-za	favourite technique
tomoenage	toh-moh-eh-na-geh	(*lit.* turning-over throw) usually translated as stomach throw
tori	toh-ri	(*lit.* the taker) the player who executes a technique
tsugiashi	t-soo-gi-ash-i	formalized walk used in *kata*. One foot leads, the other is then brought up to it but does not pass it. The first foot then takes another step
tsukuri	t-soo-koo-ri	breaking your opponent's balance
tsuri	t-soo-ri	(*lit.* fishing) common translation is pulling, as in the next throw
tsurikomiashi	t-soo-ri-koh-mi-ash-i	pulling propping ankle throw
uchikomi	uh-chi-koh-mi	(*lit.* to beat against) a form of technique training where a player practises a throw to the point where it takes effect (*kake*) without actually throwing his partner
ude	uh-deh	arm
uke	uh-keh	(*lit.* receiver) the player who is thrown or on whom a technique is applied
ukemi	uh-keh-mi	breakfall
uki	uh-ki	float or floating
ura	uh-rah	reverse
ushiro	uh-shi-roh	back or behind

Japanese word	Pronunciation	Translation
utsūri	ut-soo-ri	to change
wakare	wa-kah-reh	division or separation
waza	wa-za	technique
waza-ari	wa-za-a-ri	near technique. Usually translated as 'nearly *ippon*'
yama	ya-ma	mountain
yoko	yoh-koh	side
yon	yon	four, fourth; sometimes the word *shi* is used
yūbi	yoo-bi	finger
yūko	yoo-koh	(*lit.* effect) beats any number of *kokas*, but can itself be beaten by *waza-ari* or *ippon*
yūseigachi	yoo-seh-i-gah-chi	win by superiority. The expression given when a win is as a result of the decision made at *hantei* by referee and judges
zarei	zah-reh-i	kneeling or sitting bow
zazen	zah-zen	meditation usually done in a sitting position
zero	zeh-roh	nought
zori	zoh-ri	sandals or slippers with a central strap gripped by the toes. Traditionally made with straw but the word is now applied to any similar slipper made from all sorts of material

It is better to remember the individual words rather than complete phrases. For example, *kuzure yokoshihogatame* can be split into four words: *kuzure* meaning broken, *yoko* meaning side, *shiho* meaning four quarters and *gatame* meaning hold down.

By breaking the phrases down, as in the above example, even if you have never heard of a technique, you can get a good idea of what you are supposed to be doing. For example, something every good *judoka* should be capable of at the start of a session, particularly those with a permanently laid mat in their *dojo*, is *deharaitatami*.

INDEX